CONSCIENCE IN CONFLICT
How to Make Moral Choices

THIRD EDITION

KENNETH R. OVERBERG, S.J.

ST. ANTHONY MESSENGER PRESS

Cincinnati, Ohio

RESCRIPT

In accord with the *Code of Canon Law,* I hereby grant my permission to publish the third revised edition of *Conscience in Conflict: How to Make Moral Choices* by Kenneth R. Overberg, S.J.

Most Rev. Carl K. Moeddel
Vicar General and Auxiliary Bishop
of the Archdiocese of Cincinnati
Cincinnati, Ohio
September 6, 2005

Permission to Publish is a declaration that a book or pamphlet is considered to be free of doctrinal or moral error. It is not implied that those who have granted the Permission to Publish agree with the contents, opinions or statements expressed.

Cover and book design by Mark Sullivan
Cover photo by Duncan Walker/istockphoto

Library of Congress Cataloging-in-Publication Data
Overberg, Kenneth R.
    Conscience in conflict : how to make moral choices / Kenneth R. Overberg—3rd ed.
        p. cm.
    Includes bibliographical references and index.
    ISBN 0-86716-723-8 (pbk. : alk. paper) 1. Christian ethics—Catholic authors. 2. Decision making—Moral and ethical aspects. I. Title.

BJ1249.O92 2006
241'.042—dc22

                                                2005029283

ISBN-13 978-0-86716-723-8
ISBN-10 0-86716-723-8

Published by St. Anthony Messenger Press
28 W. Liberty St.
Cincinnati, OH 45202
www.AmericanCatholic.org

Printed in the United States of America.
Printed on acid-free paper.
06 07 08 09 10 5 4 3 2 1

*In respectful and fond memory of
Pierre Teilhard de Chardin, S.J.,
and Karl Rahner, S.J.*

contents

part one

part two

ACKNOWLEDGMENTS

This book began with a series of presentations to the first class of the Ministry Development Program in the diocese of Covington, Kentucky. I realized that what was important and helpful for these people might also be of service for a much wider audience. With these roots in Covington it seemed appropriate, then, to ask Bishop William Hughes (who has since retired) to write and now revise the Foreword. I am very pleased and honored that he did so. Thanks, Bishop Hughes!

I would also like to thank Darleen Frickman, Carol Gaeke, o.p., Mary Ann Humbert, s.c., Linda Loomis, Marianne Mione, Donna Park, Gladys Pramuk and Barbara Sheehan, s.p., who helped in a variety of ways in the preparation of this book. Thanks to Xavier University for the grant which allowed me the time for writing and to the Beckman family, whose funding of the Beckman Chair in Catholic Theology gave me time for the first revision. I remember with appreciation Jack Kramer, s.j., who has since died, for his help and interest in the book.

Finally, I want to thank St. Anthony Messenger Press, the publishers of *Catholic Update*, *Scripture From Scratch* and *St. Anthony Messenger*, for the use of materials which first appeared in those publications.

FOREWORD TO THE THIRD EDITION

Early in this twenty-first century, events in our church and world—the abuse scandal, terrorism and war, globalization, to mention a few—offer profound challenges to people of goodwill. Such events stir hearts and minds and call for careful reflection and committed action.

Other developments bring hope. More and more, members of the Catholic laity are assuming responsible positions in the church; many are becoming involved in lay pastoral ministry. And more people are trying to provide a sound moral basis to their lives. The result of many programs, such as the Cursillo, Marriage Encounter, Christ Renews His Parish and RENEW, is that many more people are seeking spiritual direction. They want a deeper personal relationship with Christ. At the core of this is a strong desire to live a good and morally responsible life.

The answers to many questions facing the church today, however, are not found simply. The gray areas and the complexity of the issues force a person to study and reflect before making moral decisions. There are no easy answers to some of these questions. There are no infallible statements that provide an easy answer for every possible inquiry.

This particular book will be very useful to any Catholic who really wants to know, "How do I, in good conscience, make moral decisions that reflect fidelity to Jesus Christ and his teachings?"

The book deals with the questions of authority, magisterium, infallibility and conscience in a balanced and respectful way. The true freedom of the individual is respected, and personal responsibility is at the core of decision-making.

Valid emphasis is placed upon the fact that one is not free to do something just because one wants to do it or because society permits it. Each individual must accept the burden of searching for the truth. This implies listening to the wisdom of authority and the guidance of its teaching, and pondering this in the light of one's own experience in an unselfish openness to God.

The author states, "The discerning method of decision-making, which recognizes the privileged guidance of the magisterium and the sanctity of conscience, rejects the extremes of blind obedience and relativism. It accepts the demands of an intelligent, informed, mature morality." This book not only provides the tools to follow such a process, but also applies those to some of the vital issues of today. The final three chapters address sexual, medical and social issues.

This book is written in understandable language, and thus should serve a wide audience among the growing number of people who are looking for help in their spiritual lives. The person who is interested in following in the footsteps of Jesus and addressing the important moral issues of the day in a responsible, informed and unselfish manner will be greatly helped by this volume.

William A. Hughes

Bishop of Covington (retired)

INTRODUCTION TO THE THIRD EDITION

Making moral decisions is a lifelong challenge. Throughout our lives we confront moral dilemmas, asking again and again, "What ought I to do?" The situations range from very intimate areas of sexuality and personal relationships to business ethics and medical issues to global questions of war and economics. We make decisions about the beginning and end of life—about artificial conception and contraception, about withdrawing life support and allowing a person to die. And we make decisions about an almost infinite number of issues in between, some major and some minor, but always regarding a dilemma which calls for a response.

Frequently, the analysis of these dilemmas proves to be most demanding. Ethical questions are rarely black or white; they are almost always gray. The staggering advancement of technology, the complexity of cultural patterns, the pluralism of lifestyles and values all make moral decisions difficult. Very often there seems to be no easy answer. Even something as simple as the decision to read this book implies saying no to some other good, such as spending this time with a friend. Other choices are much more complex: a family's decision concerning appropriate medical treatment for a dying parent, for example.

Yet moral decision-making remains a central part of our lives. Indeed, our responses shape who we are and who we are becoming—as individuals and as the human community. The complexity of moral dilemmas, therefore, is matched only by their significance. In confronting these issues, we make a statement about ourselves, affirming or denying our very humanity. Our choices and actions concerning war and drugs, abortion and racism, marriage and medicine build up or destroy our personal and communal humanity.

Although each of us must make personal moral choices, we are not completely alone. Past human experience and wisdom have been formulated into laws, both civil and religious. Indeed, for the Christian, the Scriptures and the church provide helpful guidance for moral decision-making. Helpful, but at times ambiguous, for people sometimes find conflict not only between civil and religious laws but also between church rules and their own experience and insights. Law and authority play significant roles, but do not necessarily ease the complexity of contemporary morality.

The purpose of this book, then, is to address the challenge of making moral decisions. We will reflect on the full meaning of that basic question each of us has asked so many times: "What ought I/we to do?"

Part one presents the fundamental building blocks of contemporary Catholic morality. Chapter one discusses the roots of morality in reality, along with the link between morality and spirituality. Because we are shaped by our actions, we must develop some sense of what the truly human actually is. Only then can we reflect upon the implications of our moral choices. In other words, to answer the question, "What ought I/we to do?" we must first ask, "What ought I/we to be?" (Actually, many of us simply say, "What *should* I do?" *Should* may imply, however, a false sense of obligation rooted in some external source—family or peer pressure, societal expectations and so on. *Ought* designates an authentic obligation, and so will be used throughout this book.)

After this discussion of the meaning of human life and human action, chapter two explores the process of making moral decisions. The dilemmas that face us are often complex and gray. It should not be surprising, then, if our deciding also reflects this complexity, recognizing and balancing a variety of values. Chapter three acknowledges that we are individual decision-makers who live in community. So the topic of—and possible tension between—conscience and authority is treated in some detail in this chapter, with specific attention to the question of infallibility.

Part two turns to specific moral issues of contemporary life. Chapter four focuses on sexual issues: abortion and artificial contraception and homosexuality. Chapter five treats medical issues: stem cells, euthanasia and withdrawing life-support systems, AIDS, the use of scarce resources and managed health care. Chapter six reviews the Catholic tradition of social teachings, then concentrates on the international issues of war and economics, and ends with reflections on the consistent ethic of life.

Certainly many other areas of moral concern exist in our world; clearly not all are included here. These six chapters, however, do reflect some of the major concerns and developments of Catholic moral theology since Vatican II.

An earlier revision offered the opportunity to include several major world events and recent thinking about morality, especially several official statements from the pope and the Vatican—all of which had significant impact on moral theology. The events were the breakup of the Soviet Union and the end of the

Cold War as we had experienced it for decades. Other events were the attempt to legalize physician-assisted suicide and euthanasia and the massive changes in health-care policy in the United States, especially the movement to managed care. The publications were the *Catechism of the Catholic Church* (1992) and John Paul II's encyclicals *The Splendor of Truth* (1993) and *The Gospel of Life* (1995).

The *Catechism*, as a summary of church teachings, covers most of the topics in *Conscience in Conflict*. The *Catechism* follows the renewal of Vatican II by placing its whole discussion of the moral life under the title of "Life in Christ" and by rooting its view of humanity in Scripture (the approach followed in chapter one of this text). The *Catechism*, however, follows the pattern of the earlier *Roman Catechism* (based on the Council of Trent, 1545–1563) by listing specific actions under the structure of the Ten Commandments rather than under the teachings of Jesus—the Sermon on the Mount, for example. As a result, the new *Catechism* does not always follow through on the mystery of Christ as the center of this long section (#2052–2557).

Although the *Catechism* does not always embody and express Vatican II's emphasis on the whole person understood in historical context, it provides a summary of the official teaching on most of the issues discussed in *Conscience in Conflict*. (For those interested in pursuing the links with the *Catechism*, appropriate references are given at the end of each chapter before "For Reflection and Discussion.") The mix of pre– and post–Vatican II perspectives in the *Catechism* highlights the need for a consistent ethic—both in methodology and in application to specific issues. Developing and applying such a consistent ethic is, of course, the purpose of this book.

In *The Splendor of Truth*, Pope John Paul II speaks about how people make moral decisions. He begins his reflections on moral methodology with a marvelous meditation on Jesus as the model and center of moral living. Then the pope wrestles with the problem of ethical relativism—the approach to moral decision-making that holds that each person determines the morality of an act by and for himself or herself. In contrast to this view, John Paul holds up the "splendor of truth," the conviction that reality—God, human beings and the rest of creation, all in relationship—is the basis of morality. (Part one of *Conscience in Conflict* develops this conviction in some detail.)

In this encyclical, Pope John Paul also addresses particular problems with the methodology called "proportionate reason." It is made perfectly clear in his later encyclical, *The Gospel of Life*, that the pope does not completely reject this weighing of competing values and disvalues, for he himself makes use of just such weighing when discussing end-of-life issues (see 86).

The Gospel of Life is a powerful, prophetic defense of life from womb to tomb. While concentrating on abortion and euthanasia, the pope also discusses self-defense, the death penalty and the relationship between civil and moral law. Although the encyclical does not use the phrase, it is a strong affirmation of the "consistent ethic of life," a concept first articulated by the late Cardinal Joseph Bernardin and now a centerpiece of the American bishops' teaching on the moral life.

The topics of the encyclicals correspond to the two major sections of *Conscience in Conflict*. Part one deals with moral methodology—how we make moral choices. The challenge facing contemporary Roman Catholic moral theology is how to hold together the conviction of reality as the basis of morality (as opposed to ethical relativism) with the realization that human beings can only be fully understood in their historical context (see "Characteristics of the Truly Human" in chapter one). We can grasp truth, but always from a particular perspective in space and time. The "discerning methodology" developed in part one maintains this delicate balance and, rooted in Scripture, helps us to see what best promotes human flourishing, to distinguish right and wrong.

As already indicated, part two of *Conscience in Conflict* considers some of the significant issues which confront us as individuals and as national and global communities. From the beginning of life to its end, we face many situations where we must make moral choices. In and through these decisions we choose and create what John Paul II calls "a culture of life" or "a culture of death" in *The Gospel of Life*. Our challenge is to promote life consistently.

This third edition includes new topics such as the abuse scandal, homosexuality, stem-cell research, globalization, terrorism and preemptive war.

Catholic morality has experienced a profound and rich renewal, inviting all of us into deeper love, trust, discernment and dedicated action in our day-to-day lives. Catholic morality is also threatened by rigidity and the fear of change and especially by the materialism and relativism of our culture. Rooted in our ancient Scriptures and in our rich tradition and attuned to our contemporary experience, *Conscience in Conflict* develops a vision of moral living appropriate for a new millennium.

part one

CONTEMPORARY MORAL THEOLOGY

chapter one

To Be or Not to Be

Life presents us with many moral choices. From the privacy of our personal lives to the complexity of medicine, politics and economics, issues emerge which demand decision and action. In such situations, each of us asks, "What ought I/we to do?" This question represents our first response to moral dilemmas and the beginning of ethical inquiry.

As an example of this basic question and as a case study to be discussed in these first chapters, let us consider the moral dilemma presented by Joseph Fletcher in *Situation Ethics*, first published in 1966:

> As the Russian armies drove westward to meet the Americans and British at the Elbe, a Soviet patrol picked up a Mrs. Bergmeier foraging food for her three children. Unable even to get word to the children, and without any clear reason for it, she was taken off to a prison camp in the Ukraine. Her husband had been captured in the Bulge and taken to a POW camp in Wales.
>
> When he was returned to Berlin, he spent weeks and weeks rounding up his children; two (Ilse, twelve, and Paul, ten) were found in a detention school run by the Russians, and the oldest, Hans, fifteen, was found hiding in a cellar near the Alexander Platz. Their mother's whereabouts remained a mystery, but they never stopped searching. She more than anything else was needed to re-knit them as a family in that dire situation of hunger, chaos, and fear.
>
> Meanwhile, in the Ukraine, Mrs. Bergmeier learned through a sympathetic commandant that her husband and family were trying to keep together and find her. But the rules allowed them to release her for only two reasons:
>
> (1) illness, needing medical facilities beyond the camp's, in which case she would be sent to a Soviet hospital elsewhere, and (2) pregnancy, in which case she would be returned to Germany as a liability.

She turned things over in her mind and finally asked a friendly Volga German camp guard to impregnate her, which he did. Her condition being medically verified, she was sent back to Berlin and to her family. They welcomed her with open arms, even when she told them how she had managed it. When the child was born, they loved him more than all the rest, on the view that little Dietrich had done more for them than anybody.

When it was time for him to be christened, they took him to the pastor on a Sunday afternoon. After the ceremony they sent Dietrich home with the children and sat down in the pastor's study to ask him whether they were right to feel as they did about Mrs. Bergmeier and Dietrich. Should they be grateful to the Volga German? Had Mrs. Bergmeier done a good and right thing?

Mrs. Bergmeier's case is certainly a provocative example, and we will return to it later. For now it symbolizes the fundamental moral question we all ask ourselves. (At least all who have some moral sense ask it; we judge those who do not demonstrate this moral sense to be lacking in something essential for full human life.) "What ought I/we to do?" frequently yields no easy answer. In Mrs. Bergmeier's case, no doubt, some would say she did the loving thing for the good of her family. Others would claim that she violated her marriage vows. Still others would find it difficult to come to a conclusion.

Mrs. Bergmeier's situation also highlights the many realities involved in moral decision-making. In her case, some of these are: her relationship with her husband and family, her marriage vows, her own integrity, the meaning of sexual intercourse, her relationship with the camp guard, Dietrich's relationships with other members of the family, the needs of the family and the conditions of the prison camp.

REALITY: THE BASIS OF MORALITY

How then do we answer the basic question, "What ought I/we to do?" How do we properly consider all the complex factors that make up the decision? Many possible answers have been suggested: Do that which results in the greatest good for the greatest number; do the loving thing; do what feels good.

Deeply rooted in the Catholic tradition is the conviction that morality is based on reality. Reality is God, human beings and the rest of creation—all in relationship. Every moral dilemma presents a small but real slice of this totality. The conviction that reality is the basis of morality embodies two important understandings.

First, in every situation there exists reality, a kind of objectivity, a given, something more than just an individual's sincere intentions or strong feelings. We just considered a number of realities in Mrs. Bergmeier's situation. These relationships and meanings have existence beyond what Mrs. Bergmeier feels or says about them. The same is true for all moral dilemmas. More about this emphasis later in this chapter in the section on relativism and also in chapter two.

Second, our actions help shape the kinds of persons we are becoming, and so ultimately what we ought to do is rooted in what we ought to be (that is, morality is based on the reality of our being). Because our actions shape both our very selves and also the people and the world around us, there is an intimate link between morality and existence. Our actions help determine just how truly and fully human we actually are.

Experience clearly teaches that some actions destroy our humanity. For example, murder results not only in the death of another person but also in the diminishment of the murderer's integrity. Other actions, such as love and compassion, build up our humanity.

Here is another way of saying all this. While "What ought I/we to do?" is the first question we ask, it is not the most important. Instead, it always implies a more fundamental question: "What ought I/we to be?" Only if we have some sense of what authentic human existence is can we determine if a particular action promotes or destroys this humanity.

The proper response to "What ought I/we to do?" is, then, the one which most fully respects reality and helps human life flourish in relation with God, with other human beings and with all of creation.

The realities involved in our moral choices, as was shown in the Bergmeier case, are often very complex. So moral decision-making remains a serious challenge. We will return to this topic in chapter two in order to reflect upon it in greater detail. First, however, we must work with our fundamental question, "What ought I/we to be?" (Contemporary ethics often discusses this topic under the title of "virtue ethics." See, for example, the writings of James F. Keenan, S.J., Stanley Hauerwas, Jean Porter, William C. Spohn.) Other ways to express this question are, "What is the meaning and purpose of human life?" or simply, "Who am I?"

Many different sources attempt to answer this question about the meaning of life. Psychology, anthropology, physics, sociology and philosophy all contribute their insights and perspectives. So do cultural patterns and popular media. We are profoundly influenced by some of these forces just because we live in contemporary society. For Christians, however, the most important source for helping us understand what it means to be truly human is the Bible.

But is it? The most challenging question we must ask ourselves, then, is what really grounds our values and commitments, what fills in the content of our response to "What ought I/we to be?" Is it the Bible (with special focus on the person and deeds of Jesus) or some family tradition or political and economic worldviews?

In other words, do our responses to such issues as war, welfare, abortion, capital punishment and globalization reflect a political party more than the gospel and recent Catholic teachings? How are we influenced by gender, race and class? What role do advertising and other media play in shaping our values? What are our deepest loyalties?

For an individual facing a crucial business decision, for example, the American economy may point toward maximizing profits. A perspective rooted in Scripture and the Christian tradition, however, stresses worker participation and justice. Before the business decision, then, one makes a prior choice of perspectives, a choice of which values and interpretations best enlighten the reality of the situation.

Often enough, this prior choice is actually embedded in choices about significant actions in our lives (see below the description of freedom in the section "Characteristics of the Truly Human"). We develop a set of values and commitments, a worldview, a spirituality. Our heart, this merger of spirituality and morality, provides the foundation for the response to our two basic questions.

As Richard Gula, S.S., points out in *The Call to Holiness*, we disagree on moral issues not just because of different ways of making moral decisions but because our hearts are in different places. When such differences confront each other, only a sincere openness and a careful listening to each other's stories can lead to some common ground, to some shared appreciation of reality.

The Scriptures present such a foundational worldview, recalling special encounters between God and the human family and providing the fundamental norms for living as faithful people. The Scriptures offer us some concrete moral directives. More importantly, they develop fundamental themes about the meaning of human existence. Many of the moral dilemmas facing us simply did not exist when the Scriptures were written. Neither Moses nor Jesus had to worry about test-tube babies or nuclear arms. But they did have to be concerned about authentic human life. So the Scriptures can and do give us a basic orientation about life. They tell us who God is and who the human being is. Creation and covenant in the Hebrew Scriptures, incarnation and discipleship in the Christian Scriptures: These four major biblical concepts offer a solid foundation for answering our question, "What ought I/we to be?"

CREATION AND COVENANT

The first three chapters of the book of Genesis tell us the wonderful story of creation. The rich images express extremely important convictions: that God is the source of all life, that we are created in God's image, that we are also sinful people, that we are stewards of the created world. Unlike their neighboring tribes and nations, the Hebrews came to believe in one God. Their religious experience led them to preface their own story (the patriarchs, the Exodus, the Promised Land) with the story of the very beginnings of life and the world itself (see Genesis 1:1—11:32). All comes from the one God, the source of all life.

While all creation is good, humanity is the climax of the six days of God's creating. Man and woman are created in God's own image (see Genesis 1:27). What a marvelous statement: For one another, we are an image of God! In the human we find freedom and love, compassion and creativity, reflection and imagination. In the human, by each person's very existence, there is dignity and sacredness.

These first chapters of Genesis, however, also describe another dimension of human existence: our sinfulness (see Genesis 3:1–24; also 4:1–24; 6:5–22; 11:1–9). Human freedom allows for choices and actions that contradict this image of God, that express hate and selfishness and destruction. Such evil finds embodiment not only in individuals but also in societies and cultures. Sin is inescapable, alienating people from God and from one another.

The creation story tells us not only about God as source of life and about ourselves as images of God yet sinful, but also speaks of our relationship with the rest of the created world. Continued experience and reflection on the meaning of having "dominion" (see Genesis 1:26, 28) over the world has led to a deepening awareness that we must care for the earth. Fragile and limited resources demand faithful stewardship rather than selfish and abusive appropriation.

The creation story serves as a preface to the Hebrews' foundational experience of God: the story of the Exodus and the covenant. Although Judaism claims Abraham as its "father in faith," the Exodus story describes Moses as first molding Abraham's descendants as well as other Semitic tribes into the nation of Israel. After recalling the birth, early life and call of Moses, the book of Exodus narrates the Hebrews' escape from Egypt (see Exodus 12:1—14:31). The story is familiar: the plagues; the Hebrews being led by God, described as a pillar of fire and a pillar of cloud; the Egyptians chasing after the Hebrews; the parting of the sea that allowed the Hebrews to escape and then the waters destroying the Egyptians.

It is a story rich in symbol. Although the Exodus experience of God's liberation occurred in the thirteenth century B.C.E., the story was not written down until hundreds of years later. In between, as the people settled in the Promised Land, Canaan, they developed rituals to celebrate the special events of their history. When the first books of the Bible were finally composed, the writers combined the later ritual development with the original experience in order to remember and hand on the Exodus experience (the Passover feast). Of course, the writers also had to use symbols (such as the pillar of fire) to try to describe God's presence and action in the Exodus.

What historical fact lies behind the Exodus story? The Hebrews were oppressed and they did escape to freedom. What was of greatest importance for the people, however, was the fact that this refugee experience was also a religious experience, a special encounter with God, who was active in their history and delivered them to freedom (see Exodus 14:14, 21, 27).

God's choice of the Hebrews is ratified in a solemn agreement, the covenant. After presenting some of the trials a refugee people faces in the desert (lack of food and water, battles with foreign peoples) and evidence of God's care for them, the book of Exodus describes the sacred experience at Mount Sinai

(19:1—24:18). The encounter is marvelously described:

> On the morning of the third day there was thunder and light-
> ning, as well as a thick cloud on the mountain, and a blast of
> a trumpet so loud that all the people who were in the camp
> trembled. Moses brought the people out of the camp to meet
> God. They took their stand at the foot of the mountain. Now
> Mount Sinai was wrapped in smoke, because the LORD had
> descended upon it in fire; the smoke went up like the smoke
> of a kiln, while the whole mountain shook violently. As the
> blast of the trumpet grew louder and louder, Moses would
> speak and God would answer him in thunder. When the
> LORD descended upon Mount Sinai, to the top of the moun-
> tain, the LORD summoned Moses to the top of the mountain,
> and Moses went up. (Exodus 19:16–20)

Through Moses God establishes a special bond with the Hebrew people. This people is chosen as God's very own and they respond with complete commitment. God will be their God and will continue to protect them; the people will show their commitment by keeping God's law. In this solemn context Moses receives the Ten Commandments and many other laws and regulations.

In the symbolic ratification of this covenant, Moses pours blood on an altar and sprinkles it on the people (see Exodus 24:4–8). For the Hebrews, blood was a symbol for the very life of a being. By sprinkling blood on the altar (which represents God) and on the people, Moses symbolically expresses the conviction that the covenant partners (God and the people) share a common life.

As Christians, our roots are also in the Hebrew Scriptures. The story of the Hebrew people is our story. The Hebrew Scriptures then help us to understand the full meaning of human life. All life is a gift given by our Creator God; all life is fundamentally good. Human life in particular reflects the image of God; human love and thought and compassion and freedom reveal different dimensions of God. As such each human life is sacred and possesses a dignity based not on what one can do but simply on one's very existence. Human life is essentially communal; life is to be lived with others.

Human life is also sinful. By our free choices and actions we can alienate ourselves from God and from other people and from the earth. Therefore one goal of authentic life is to overcome this alienation. Rejecting sin is possible because of God's continuing care and compassion. Our God did not stop with creation but is active in history, freeing us from oppression and choosing us as God's very own people.

INCARNATION AND DISCIPLESHIP

As Christians, we also believe in the new covenant in Jesus. So we turn to the New Testament, looking for even more answers to "What ought I/we to be?" Again we find a number of specific regulations; more importantly, we find in Jesus the complete embodiment of fully human life.

The New Testament, like the Old Testament, is an account of faith whose purpose is to tell us of God's action in the world, but not to give an exact historical or scientific account of events. As a result, when we read the Christian Scriptures, it is helpful to remember that they were written decades after the Resurrection in order to proclaim Jesus as Lord and Savior. The new insight and understanding that resulted from the resurrection experience colored the way the stories of Jesus were told.

By keeping in mind this resurrection focus while listening to what the early Christian community said about him, we can gain some insight into Jesus of Nazareth.

Jesus' life was grounded in a very intimate, loving relationship with God. Undoubtedly, this bond developed gradually as Jesus lived, read the Hebrew Scriptures, began his own prophetic ministry and took time to be alone and pray. Jesus expressed this intimate relationship by using the word *Abba* for God. Some Scripture scholars say that Jesus chose this word that small children used to address their fathers to convey a sense of childlike simplicity and familiarity. Other scholars have offered the image of patron for understanding Jesus' use of the word. Appreciating the cultural world of the first century suggests this alternative interpretation, which implies a mature personal relationship with the one who empowers and distributes benefits, emphasizing trust, responsibility and fidelity. Jesus also expressed his intimate relationship with God in his parables, describing God as a gentle and forgiving parent in the story of the Prodigal Son, for example.

In his teachings Jesus described the reign of God, communicating some sense of what God's loving presence means for individuals and society. In the

Sermon on the Mount (Matthew 5:1—7:29), we discover some of the joy, surprise and goodness of the reign of God: The hungry will be satisfied; those who weep will laugh; the poor will be part of the reign. We also hear other characteristics of life in the reign of God: love of enemies, generosity, compassion, forgiveness, trust and faithful action.

The Gospels describe Jesus exemplifying these characteristics in his encounters with people and in his own passion and death. Just as he steadfastly journeyed to Jerusalem, so in his passion Jesus prayed in the garden and calmly faced death. Just as he described mercy and tenderness in his parables and expressed them in his actions, so Jesus forgave those who crucified him. Just as he taught about *Abba*, so at death Jesus entrusted his spirit into *Abba's* hands. Finally, Jesus' intimate, loving relationship was confirmed by *Abba's* power, which raised Jesus to new life. The Resurrection can be understood as God's affirmation of Jesus' faithfulness, as the definitive triumph of life over death.

As Christians, we believe that Jesus is both divine and human, the revelation of God's love and human response. As Christians, we are called to be Jesus' disciples, modeling our lives on his. Discipleship takes its meaning from Jesus' life. The characteristics expressed in his life and teachings are the foundation of discipleship: commitment, intimacy, compassion, forgiveness, care for the poor and outcast, faithful action, trust. Jesus, then, offers us the best example of authentic human life.

CREATION FOR THE SAKE OF INCARNATION

Because the life, death and resurrection of Jesus make up the foundation of Christianity, the Christian community has long reflected on their significance for our lives. What was the purpose of Jesus' life?

Within the Christian tradition, there have been a variety of attempts to answer this question. One view, deeply rooted in Scripture and probably most frequently handed on in everyday religion, is the understanding of Jesus' life that emphasizes redemption. This view returns to the creation story and sees in Adam and Eve's sin a fundamental alienation from God, a separation so profound that God must intervene to overcome it. The Incarnation, the Word becoming flesh, is considered as God's action to right this original wrong. Redemption, then, is basically understood as a "buying back."

Popular piety has often expressed redemption in terms of "opening the gates of heaven" and Jesus "making up" for our sinfulness. This focus has especially centered on Jesus' passion and death, at times seeming to imply that an angry God demanded the Son's suffering as a necessary placating act. The purpose of Jesus' life is directly linked to original sin and all human sinfulness. Jesus, particularly by his passion and death, buys us back. Without original sin, there would have been no need for the Incarnation.

There exists, however, another perspective on the purpose of Jesus' life. Founded on John's Gospel and other New Testament writings and developed throughout the Christian tradition, this view emphasizes the Incarnation. God so loved the world that God gave the only Son, so that everyone who believes in him might have eternal life (see John 3:16). The Word became flesh not to suffer but to live and to share divine love. John's Gospel does not see Jesus' life and death as atonement or a ransom (unlike the Synoptic Gospels, for example Mark 10:45). There is instead emphasis on friendship, intimacy, mutuality, service, faithful love—revealing God's desire and gift for the full flourishing of humanity, or in other words, salvation (see the Farewell Address, John 13:1—17:26).

John's meditation on God's supreme act of love in the Incarnation (see John 1:1–18) provides the heart of this vision: The whole purpose of creation is for the Incarnation. Jesus' life fulfills God's eternal longing to become human, to share life and love in a unique and definitive way. For many of us who have lived a lifetime with the atonement view, it may be hard at first to hear this alternate view. Yet it may offer some wonderful surprises for our relationships with God and others.

This alternate view offers us a new and transformed image of God. God's overflowing love, the very life of the Trinity, is expressed in creation, Incarnation and final fulfillment. Incarnation is God's first thought, the original design for all creation. From this perspective, God is appreciated with a different emphasis. God is not an angry or vindictive God, demanding the suffering and death of Jesus as a payment for past sin. God is, instead, a gracious God, sharing divine life and love in creation and in the Incarnation (like parents sharing their love in the life of a new child).

The focus on the Word made flesh helps us to appreciate the depth of our humanness and the importance of our actions. Jesuit Karl Rahner's marvelous musings on our life in a world of grace give us renewed understanding of the biblical phrase "created in God's image"—along with many implications for how we treat all our sisters and brothers in the human family and the earth itself. Creation itself is understood to be very good. Sin is recognized, but creation is not totally corrupted as a result. Creation is the gift of this gracious God, and so we can expect to find hints of God in creation, especially in human beings. Creation is a source of revelation.

The perspective of creation-for-Incarnation highlights the rich meaning of Jesus. Jesus is not just an afterthought. He is not Plan B, sent simply to make up for sin. As Franciscan John Duns Scotus emphasized so well, God's masterpiece, Jesus, must result from something much greater and more positive (God's desire to share life and love). Jesus is the culmination of God's self-gift to the world. Jesus, then, is the model of full human life, the answer to "What ought I/we to be?"

Vatican II and Human Dignity

The fundamental biblical themes of creation and covenant, incarnation and discipleship help us to know the meaning of human life. They are timeless. But because human beings always live in a particular time and culture, insights into the meaning of life are always influenced by that time and culture. It may be necessary, then, as times and cultures change, to find new ways to express religious insights and convictions about life. What was appropriate and helpful in the Middle Ages may require different articulation at the beginning of a new millennium. We must keep these biblical insights in dialogue with our ongoing experience in the world, with science and technology and all forms of new knowledge.

The Second Vatican Council (1962–1965) is well known for its efforts to read the signs of the times and to rephrase the fundamental truths of Christianity. Especially in its *Pastoral Constitution on the Church in the Modern World*, Vatican II presented a "theological anthropology," that is, a description rooted in the Scriptures of what it means to be truly human.

> The people of God believes that it is led by the Spirit of the
> Lord who fills the whole world. Impelled by that faith, it tries
> to discern in the events, the needs, and the longings which it

shares with humans of our time, what may be genuine signs of the presence or of the purpose of God. For faith throws a new light on all things and makes known the full ideal which God has set for humanity, thus guiding the mind towards solutions that are fully human. (11)

The dignity of the person provides the basis for the document's responses to the crises resulting from profound changes in culture, society, politics and religion. This dignity is rooted in our creation in God's image, a dignity fully revealed in Jesus Christ. The human being is essentially social, created for interpersonal communion and for knowledge and love of the Creator. The human being is one, made up of body and spirit. Possessing intelligence and freedom, the person seeks wisdom and truth and is summoned by conscience to love good and avoid evil.

The document recognizes evil in the world. All human life, whether individual or collective, is involved in a dramatic struggle between good and evil. But sin is overcome in Jesus Christ. The human being is redeemed by Christ and made a new creature:

> The Church believes that Christ, who died and was raised for the sake of all, can show people the way and strengthen them through the Spirit so that they become worthy of their destiny....The Church likewise believes that the key, the center and the purpose of the whole of human history is to be found in its Lord and Master....And that is why the Council, relying on the inspiration of Christ, the image of the invisible God, the firstborn of all creation, proposes to speak to all people in order to unfold the mystery that is humankind and cooperate in tackling the main problems facing the world today. (10)

With this sense of the meaning of human life, the *Pastoral Constitution on the Church in the Modern World* can then address specific issues of marriage and family, social and economic life, war and peace. In so doing, the document reminds us that in order to answer the specific moral question, "What ought I/we to do?" we must ask the prior question, "What ought I/we to be?"

Characteristics of the Truly Human

For Christians, the Bible is the most important source for answering this question, but not the only source. All the valid insights of the various arts and sciences, along with ordinary human experience, help in describing what it means to be truly human. Vatican II was one example of combining these various insights with a theological perspective. Another example is the work of the great Jesuit theologian Karl Rahner (1904–1984).

Rahner wrote extensively and played a major role in the renewal of Catholic theology. Among his many interests was the attempt to describe the truly human. Combining a vast knowledge of the Christian tradition with the transcendental method of philosophy (a method which reflects upon what is implicitly affirmed about existence in every act of knowing and loving) and with attention to human experience, Rahner developed six basic characteristics of what it means to be human. He was convinced that these characteristics were true for all people, common qualities not limited to a particular time or culture. Clearly, these characteristics are valuable in establishing the foundation of a contemporary Catholic morality.

1) *Embodiment.* The first characteristic is that we are body people. To be human is to be embodied. We are incarnate; we are people existing in a particular time and place. We cannot not be body people! (We have been discussing the importance of the "to be" question for the "to do" one. Perhaps a brief example, based on this characteristic, will clarify this discussion. If to be human necessarily implies being embodied, then we have an obligation to take care of our body. We cannot just arbitrarily cut off an arm, for instance. That "to do"—cutting off an arm for no good reason—contradicts our "to be"— being fully human.)

To be embodied necessarily means that we exist in a particular time and place and culture. This point, which may appear obvious, has important implications for moral theology. Because we exist in time, our culture shapes us and we shape our culture. That we exist at the beginning of a new millennium influences both the way we think and the issues we confront. We cannot escape that influence. It does not absolutely determine us, but it does have an impact on us. Because we cannot stand outside of time and place and culture, we cannot develop a completely objective view of this reality. We always remain in the midst of it, experiencing its influence.

As time and cultures change, then, humanity may also change. (Just compare our lives today with those of our ancestors many thousands of years ago.) To be rooted in history is to be shaped in part by history. Therefore, this first characteristic of our humanity, embodiment, means that one of the unchangeable aspects of being human is that we are open to change. This point is especially important for Catholic moral theology. Vatican II called for a renewal of moral theology based on greater emphasis on Scripture and on the whole person. For a long time the Catholic tradition had not sufficiently appreciated the possibility of change. Instead, it emphasized the unchanging, the objective. This perspective considered the basic structures of human life as fixed and knowable. In a sense it possessed all the answers, which simply had to be applied to the particular situation and expressed in concrete moral norms.

An openness to change, on the other hand, does recognize the ambiguity of moral issues and the dynamism of life. It also recognizes the difficulty in determining just what is truly human. (The area of medical ethics is an excellent example of this tension: Genetic engineering may help eliminate hereditary diseases, but it may also undermine our humanity by attempting to create a super race.) It does not, however, mean that everything is up for grabs or that each person individually determines the morality of a situation. (This form of ethics, relativism, will be discussed in greater detail later in this chapter.) There is still a reality, a moral situation, which is either destructive or constructive of the truly human. Our task, while acknowledging our roots in a particular time and place, is to discern the meaning of that reality.

This whole discussion about time and culture shaping who we are is rooted in Rahner's first characteristic, the apparently simple fact that we are body people.

2) *Spirituality.* The second characteristic common to all people is that, besides body, we are also spirit. We are not limited to our bodies, not completely immersed in the world. We do not act merely out of instinct. Instead, we are reflective beings, persons who can think—even debate with ourselves—about our actions. We ask ourselves, "What ought I/we to do?" We determine answers and then act. We are doers. Just as we cannot step outside time and place to view reality, so we cannot step outside our own subjectivity to view ourselves. We can never have a perfectly objective picture of ourselves because we are always doing the looking; we are always subjects. As spirit, we also reach

beyond ourselves in knowledge and in love. We experience a sense of transcendence: There is more to know and to love, yet we can never fully attain this unlimited reality. As spirit, we find ourselves incomplete, open to and striving for something more.

3) *Solidarity.* As body-spirit people, we are also social. This third characteristic of human existence implies that to be human is to be in relationship with other people. We are community builders, not isolated islands. We are interdependent. We are not in total control of our lives, but are affected by other people and events. Clearly this quality has important applications not only to understanding the human but also to interpreting worldwide political, economic and social responsibilities. To exist is to be part of the whole human family. We are in relationship with relatives and friends, of course, but also with all other human beings.

4) *Uniqueness.* We are also unique. Even though we share the common qualities of being body, spirit and social beings, each of us is an individual. Rahner's fourth characteristic indicates that each human being is more than just the sum total of genes, family relationships and cultural influences. Even identical twins are different persons; each is unique.

5) *Freedom.* Rahner's fifth characteristic, freedom, especially requires careful analysis. Rahner acknowledges the many limits placed on us by culture and society and family. He shows, however, that a fundamental freedom exists at our very core. This freedom is our capacity to choose whether or not to be truly human, the freedom of self-realization. In other words, we are free "to be or not to be."

Indeed, the "to be or not to be" decision is the fundamental ethical choice of our lives. We do not make such a decision in the abstract but in and through decisions about significant actions in our lives. Again, our "doing" shapes our "being." As we move along through life, we confront major issues: vocation, fidelity, justice, to name a few. Our choices and actions in these situations also help shape our very selves; these choices and actions either promote or undermine our humanity. By our concrete choices, we define the meaning of life and set a course for our own lives, either affirming or denying the truly human. This capacity to shape ourselves, to determine the direction of our lives, is what Rahner means by fundamental freedom.

6) *Capacity for relationship with God.* Rahner states that these five characteristics—that we are body, spirit, social, unique and free—are qualities inherent in human nature. There is another characteristic common to all humans but not part of human nature as such: our capacity to be in relationship with God.

Humans are capable of encountering God; they are called to personal communion with God. Rahner contends that this quality of human existence is found in all, not by nature of their being human but only as a gift of God. Rahner uses a technical name for this characteristic: "the supernatural existential." By existential Rahner means this dimension is given in all of us, that we are simply built that way (just like being unique and social). By supernatural he means that this characteristic is not ours by right of our nature (that is, we would be human without it) but only as a result of God's graciousness.

Rahner holds that this gift is given to all humans, so that pure human nature does not exist, only graced human nature. Therefore, in the real world of graced human nature, to be truly human includes being in relationship with God. Rahner stresses that people can still be open to God even if they have never heard of God by refusing to make a god out of some limited reality (money or power or success, for example). The choice for the truly human implicitly affirms one's relationship with God.

THE MEANING OF HUMAN EXISTENCE

In this chapter, we have been considering the fundamental ethical dilemma: to be or not to be. Through our significant choices, we shape our very selves; we nurture or destroy our humanity. Morality, then, is based on reality. What I ought to do is rooted in what I ought to be. Scripture and contemporary reflection provide important insights into the meaning of human existence. To be human includes being in relationship with God. For some of us this relationship is made explicit in the covenant experience. We are God's people and disciples of Jesus; intimacy and trust, compassion and forgiveness, faithful action and concern for justice characterize our lives. Each person is recognized as an image of God, and therefore sacred and special. To be human is to be body and spirit, individual and social. To be human is to possess the awesome capacity to say yes or no to this reality.

Moral choices are those that promote this reality. Understanding reality is not a simple task, however. Because we are historical people and because we participate in various communities (religious, economic, political, social) with different—even conflicting—values, not only are the moral choices complex, but even the meaning of human existence is open to different interpretations. (We will return to this topic in chapter three.)

Three other issues are related to this conviction that reality is the basis of morality and worthy of consideration in this chapter: grace, sin and relativism.

GRACE

We have already considered the fundamentals for our understanding of grace. God's graciousness is expressed in creation, in the depths of each person and in Jesus of Nazareth. Divine love is so great that God desired to share that love in creating the universe. God sees all creation as good. Indeed, creation reflects the Creator; hints of God can be found in all aspects of life.

For some people, nature provides the perfect setting for encountering God. In pondering the awesomeness of creation—the power of oceans, the beauty of sunsets, the majesty of mountains—these people claim to be aware of God. Another ordinary experience that can become an experience of grace is love and friendship. As expressed in Genesis, human beings are indeed seen to be images of God. People find God in the depth of love between wife and husband, in the wonder of a parent's love for a child, in the steadfast love of true friends. A third example of creation's capacity to reveal God is, somewhat surprisingly, the dark side of life. Sickness, all kinds of tragedy and death itself allow people to encounter the Mystery which is in all and surpasses all. Separation and oppression, mental illness and terrorism, starvation and threats of war are overwhelming and yet also, at times, grace-filled.

We also find grace at the core of our being. As so eloquently described by Rahner, God's graciousness is expressed in the very structure of our being. As human beings, we reach out to know more and to love more. Our minds and hearts are never fully satisfied by any created reality. We are finite beings with an infinite capacity. We feel made for something more, yet we cannot reach our goal alone. Only God, the Infinite, can fulfill our deepest human yearnings.

To be human, then, is to be open to and in relationship with God, holy Mystery. Just as we are social beings, built to be in relationships with other people, so, too, we are built to be in relationship with God. Fulfillment of our potential for human relationships depends both on others' initiative and on our response. In a similar way, our relationship with God depends on God's initiative and our response. As we just saw, God's initiative comes to us through the ordinary experiences of life.

God's graciousness has also been expressed in a special way in Jesus. As we saw earlier in the section on the Incarnation (see pages 10 to 13), Jesus can be validly understood as the full, final and irrevocable event of God's self-communication. Jesus reveals God's love and the authentic human response to that love. We, as Jesus' disciples, continue to live and proclaim that Good News.

Understanding reality necessarily includes an appreciation of grace. Grace is God's initiative, God's inviting us to an intimate, loving relationship and empowering us to respond to this invitation. Grace is God's self-communication. In our graced world, we experience God's initiative in ourselves, in the people and events of our world, in Jesus Christ.

SIN

If grace speaks of our loving relationship with God, then sin is the breaking of that relationship. Sin occurs when we contradict what it means to be truly human, when in some act that expresses our fundamental freedom we deny an essential dimension of our humanity. For example, deliberately to hold and foster hatred toward another race would be a sinful choice, contradicting the social characteristic of our humanity. Denying our own humanity destroys our relationship with God. Our relationship with God, whether expressed explicitly or not, is always embedded in the choices which express our fundamental freedom.

Just as those who have never heard of God can affirm God by their choice of the truly human, so, too, we can deny God by sinful choices even though we never mention God. Sin, at its root, is saying no to God's invitation to a loving relationship. Sin alienates us from God, from others, from our true selves.

Sin is a contradiction. Our freedom stems from God as the ground of all our experience, yet sin denies God. Our very being is built to be in relationship with God; only God can fulfill the human. Sin, however, claims the opposite: that something finite—power or pleasure or money—can satisfy the deepest human yearnings.

Sin is not merely the breaking of a law. Sin is the breaking of a relationship. Laws were formulated in light of experience to help us appreciate what destroys or promotes our humanity. Laws (as we will see in greater detail later in this book) provide guidance. Violation of the law is not the significant point; destruction of the human is. To sin is to choose not to be fully human.

Relativism

The other issue requiring discussion in light of the conviction that reality is the ground of morality is the opposite conviction: ethical relativism. In our culture, relativism is rampant, almost in the air we breathe. Relativism is the approach to ethical dilemmas which says that each individual determines the morality of a particular situation. An act may not be moral for me, but it is for you (abortion, for example). No one can tell another what is moral.

While there is some truth in the statement that each person must decide (as we will see when we discuss conscience in chapter three), our decision does not constitute the morality of the situation. Instead, the reality itself—whether the act promotes or destroys the truly human—is the basis of morality. This conviction clearly opposes relativism.

As we noted earlier, understanding reality is not necessarily an easy task. Long ago, the human community reached the obvious conclusion that killing is destructive of humanity. Many other issues, genetic engineering, for example, may not be as clear to us. This ambiguity, along with the recognition that we are historical people and so open to change, only emphasizes our responsibility to search continuously for insight into what builds up the fully human and what destroys it. Only then can we determine what we ought to do.

Summing Up

Our ethical inquiry begins when life presents us with moral dilemmas and we ask, "What ought I/we to do?" In order to answer this question, we must first ask a prior question, "What ought I/we to be?" Scripture, the Christian tradition and reflection on human experience help us to appreciate the truly human. Insight into the various dimensions of our humanity provides us with the basis for judging the morality of actions. We now can consider the process of making moral decisions.

Catechism References
Nos. 1691–1748, 1803–1896, 1987–2029.

FOR REFLECTION AND DISCUSSION

1. Reflect on significant moral choices you have made in your life. What elements particularly influenced your decision: Scripture, church law, peer pressure, your own experience? Did your choices promote or undermine your humanity? Would you approach the choice differently now?

2. What Scripture passages are your favorites? How do they give direction to your moral decision-making? What experiences in your life embody the biblical themes of covenant and discipleship? How do these experiences help to answer the basic question: "What ought I/we to be?"

3. What experiences in your life affirm Rahner's characteristics of the truly human? What changes have you seen in the world in your lifetime? In yourself? How has your freedom to choose shaped the person you are today?

4. Reflect on the importance of trust, compassion and concern for justice in your life. What other—even conflicting—values does our culture promote? How are these values communicated?

5. How does the concept of "creation for the sake of Incarnation" affect your image of God? How have you experienced grace? Reflect on personal sin and the oppressive ("sinful") structures of society. How do these contradict the biblical themes? How is that different from breaking a law?

6. Give examples of relativism at work in our culture. How does morality based on reality oppose relativism? What realities were present in the moral choices you recalled in Question 1? What realities were involved in Mrs. Bergmeier's decision? In light of this chapter, what do you think Mrs. Bergmeier ought to have done? Why?

chapter two

M A K I N G   M O R A L   D E C I S I O N S

Choosing the action that most fully promotes our humanity is no easy task. Moral dilemmas confront us with profound complexity. Values rooted in different worldviews offer conflicting interpretations of reality. Some persons, for example, judge artificial conception (test-tube fertilization) to be contrary to human nature, while others see it as a compassionate use of technology to help nature. Our culture suggests a variety of means of resolving these difficulties. In this chapter, therefore, we will carefully consider the process of making moral decisions, the process of answering our initial question, "What ought I/we to do?"

In chapter one, Mrs. Bergmeier's situation symbolized the complexity of many moral dilemmas. We could add many examples from our own experience. Often we find that a decision seems to promote one good but deny another. Even when we recognize the need to consider the question "What ought I/we to be?" opposing worldviews present very different interpretations of the meaning of life. In chapter one we reflected on the significance of Scripture, the Christian tradition and human experience for moral theology.

Much, however, remains to be considered in the process of making moral decisions. "What ought I/we to do?" almost always raises conflicts for us. Very few if any of our decisions are between absolute good and absolute evil. Instead, life presents us with situations where decisions are not so clear-cut. For example, your decision to work in a soup kitchen means that you will spend less time with your family, reading a book or planting a garden. A business decision may result in greater profit but less justice for the worker. Saying yes to one perceived good often means saying no to another.

How do we deal with this kind of conflict? How do we answer our question, "What ought I/we to do?" Generally, three approaches have been suggested: (1) the teleological (from the Greek *telos*, "goal" or "end"), (2) the deontological (from the Greek *deon*, "duty" or "obligation") and (3) the discerning (also called the "responsibility" or "revisionist" model).

The teleological approach concentrates on the particular situation and tells the decision-maker to look at the goal or consequences. A decision can then be made in light of some directive: Do the greatest good for the greatest number, for example, or do the loving thing. We have already seen in chapter one the limits of this approach, especially its failure to recognize that morality is rooted in reality, to acknowledge the common elements of our humanity and the wisdom of past experience as expressed in law.

The deontological approach begins with the basic values of human life (such as telling the truth) and holds that we cannot act directly against these values. This method holds that some human acts are morally right or wrong no matter what the consequences. The deontological approach then formulates laws that become the basis for judging the morality of a particular act. This method invests great confidence in the role and scope of law, and so concentrates on duty and obligation.

As we saw in chapter one, however, human reality is open to change as time and cultures change. Such shifts give rise to a needed change in the law. Vatican II provided a dramatic example of this change in its document on religious liberty, unambiguously acknowledging for the first time the individual's right and responsibility to follow one's conscience concerning religion. Another limitation to the deontological approach is the difficulty in formulating laws to cover the great variety of moral dilemmas that confront us. Medical issues, for example, include so many complexities and possible conflicts of basic goods that making appropriately finely tuned norms is practically impossible.

The discerning approach attempts to combine the value and wisdom of law (rooted in reality) with the uniqueness of concrete situations. Rooted in reality, this approach avoids relativism on the one hand; accepting the significance of the concrete situation, it avoids blind obedience to law on the other. This discerning approach, though certainly not the easiest, best respects the complexities of life in answering our question, "What ought I/we to do?"

THE AMPUTATION

An example will help clarify this method of making moral decisions. Imagine that you sit down to view a video that depicts a surgeon cutting off a person's arm. We can ask, "Is this an action that ought to be done?" We cannot, however, answer that question completely. We need more information. Indeed, first we must move to our deeper level of the meaning of reality. We recall that we are body people, that we have a responsibility to preserve and nurture our bodies. Therefore, to cut off an arm is not a good thing; ordinarily, it is an action that ought not to be done.

Still, we are unable to make a moral judgment about the action on our video. Clearly, we need to know *why* the amputation is being done. Even though we are body people and so need to preserve the integrity of our bodies, there may be a serious reason for the amputation. If the arm is full of gangrene and all medications have failed, then the amputation may be necessary to save the individual's life. In this case, a greater value—life itself—outweighs the value of having two arms. We would then judge the amputation as an act that ought to be done, a moral act.

If the arm were perfectly sound, however, but was being cut off as an act of torture or as a means of removing a hangnail (to be ridiculous), then we would say that the act ought not to be done, that it was immoral (that is, it would diminish or destroy the humanity of the surgeon).

Most of our moral decisions are more complex. But the example, because it is so simple, helps to clarify this discerning method of making moral decisions. Only the understanding of reality and of the particular circumstances, including intentions and consequences, can yield a moral decision.

The pivotal point, obviously, is the question of sufficient reason. Not just any reason, even an important or strongly felt one, qualifies as a *sufficient* reason. Rather, a reason is sufficient when the act supports the value in question and does not contradict or undermine it. In this example, amputation (an act which ordinarily ought not to be done) actually supported the basic value (respect for bodily life) in the case of gangrene. In the hangnail situation, amputation would contradict the value.

Premoral and Moral Evil

In the case above, because of our conviction that reality is the basis of morality (in this situation, the fact that we are people with bodies), we recognized the value of physical integrity. Thus, an amputation can rightly be called an evil. But until we knew all the circumstances, we could not judge whether the act is immoral. The term used to describe such an act is *premoral* evil.

It is very important to note that evil does not necessarily imply something immoral. When we hear the word we should not automatically think "moral evil"—even though we usually do that! More precision in our language is necessary for careful moral reasoning. We need to qualify evil; we need to determine whether it is premoral evil or moral evil.

Premoral evil is destructive of some aspect of who we are, of what it means to be truly human. Therefore, such things as suffering, ignorance, sickness and death can be considered premoral evil. Such realities are damaging or destructive, at least in a physical sense, to the human person. But these realities remain premoral evil until all the necessary conditions are considered.

Moral evil is premoral evil that is committed without a sufficient reason. Moral evil destroys our very humanity and in so doing breaks our relationship with God. In the video, the amputation is premoral evil. What makes the difference in terms of morality is the total situation. To save a life is clearly a sufficient reason to cut off an arm. To torture someone or to remove a hangnail is clearly not a sufficient reason. In such a case the amputation would be judged to be an immoral act.

Notice the two steps. First, we look to the reality of the situation. Revelation, philosophy, the sciences, our experience all help us understand whether some act is evil—that is, destructive or damaging of the truly human. Second, we look at the total reality, including circumstances and intentions and consequences, in order to judge whether there is a sufficient reason for causing some premoral evil. Only then can we determine whether it is moral evil.

The case of amputation was fairly simple. Most would agree that saving a life is worth removing an arm; getting rid of a hangnail is not. While the example helps clarify the methodology, however, we also recognize that most of our moral dilemmas are more complicated. Just think of Mrs. Bergmeier. How would she balance justifying reasons against the evil involved? (We will attempt to answer that question later in this chapter.) Making moral decisions, then, is a challenging task. Chapter one helped us with the first step, understanding the reality of the situation. The distinction between premoral evil and moral evil provides added insight. Still we must consider in greater detail what constitutes a sufficient reason.

CRITERIA FOR DISCERNMENT

The highly respected moral theologian Richard McCormick, S.J., who had long been involved in this discussion, outlined a very demanding process of reflection. In *Ambiguity in Moral Choice*, he describes six criteria for determining a sufficient reason:

We are to *weigh the social implications* of the act we are considering. Clearly not everything can be predicted, but a serious look at consequences for ourselves and others is to be included.

We are to *use the test of generalizability*. Even though we are tempted to think that we are absolutely unique, we are to recognize our shared humanity and ask what would happen if our act became a norm for all.

We are to *reflect on cultural influences*, particularly how they might bias our judgment.

We are to *learn from the wisdom of past human experience*, especially as this has been embodied in laws that have provided sound guidance.

We are to *consult broadly*, aware that our own self-interest might color our judgment and aware that others have special expertise and insight.

We are to *make full use of our religious beliefs*, allowing them to enlighten the reality of our moral dilemma.

McCormick further reminds us that this search for sufficient reason to cause premoral evil is necessarily communal. Weighing values in conflict cannot be done in an individualistic way (though this is certainly one of our cultural biases). The criteria clearly express the need for extensive consultation with tradition, authority, various experts and people sensitive to human experience. This reflection is properly called discernment, for it is much more than some quantitative exercise, a mere adding and subtracting. It is a prudential and prayerful weighing of fundamental—and at times seemingly conflicting—goods (again, recall the complexity of Mrs. Bergmeier's decision).

This way of answering our question "What ought I/we to do?" leads to a mature morality. Neither self-centered individualism nor blind obedience to law respect the dignity and calling of the human being. This discerning methodology does, accepting reality as the basis of morality and acknowledging the significance of the circumstances, intentions and consequences of moral dilemmas.

This process requires the intelligent and reflective participation of the moral decision-maker. It may also raise some concerns—about its method, about the law, about tradition. We turn now to a careful consideration of each of these concerns and so to a deeper understanding of this way of making moral decisions.

OF ENDS AND MEANS

The discerning method may raise the question: Does the end justify the means? This issue has long been debated. Some approaches to ethics (the teleological) assume as the fundamental principle for making moral decisions that the end justifies the means. Politics and business provide many examples of this kind of thinking. If success is a particular end or goal, then whatever means help attain that end—including lying and cheating—are acceptable. Other approaches (the deontological) reject this position, judging that evil acts seem to be thereby justified.

The discerning methodology outlined in this chapter responds with a no and a yes to the question of whether the end justifies the means. Some nuancing is clearly necessary!

As we have seen, this method rejects pure situation ethics both in its conviction that reality is the basis for morality and in its affirmation that not every reason suffices to cause premoral evil. Simply to state that the end justifies the means is not sufficient, and so our method rejects this view.

On the other hand, there is a sense in which we can affirm that the end does justify the means. Indeed, that is the only way we can reach a decision about a moral dilemma. In the video example, the means (the amputation) was the same in both cases. The deciding difference was the end, the purpose of the action. To claim that the end justifies the means is rightly interpreted as the careful discernment of the values to be achieved as outweighing (not in our desire, but in reality) the disvalues involved. This methodology, then, holds together both the affirmation of reality as the basis for morality and the acceptance of the end justifying the means (understood properly).

Critics of the discerning methodology have claimed that it undermines the law, permitting such evils as injustice and even murder. This criticism often seems to be grounded in misinterpretation of the question concerning ends and means. The critics judge that the discerning method uses the purely situational interpretation: "The end justifies the means." In fact, as we have seen, attention to the situation is only part of the process. This method begins with the conviction that morality is rooted in reality and that not every reason is sufficient to cause premoral evil. Our responsibility, then, is to discern the realities involved (what enhances our humanity, what dehumanizes us) and balance the good that will be achieved against the premoral evil that will be caused.

What can be said of the relationship between this method and the law? First, the discerning method in no way contradicts the law. Instead, properly understood, the method is the foundation of the law. All laws, including the Ten Commandments and all the others expressed in Scripture, are rooted in human experience. People have lived and reflected on the events of life in light of their relationship with God. Such experience, reflection and faith led these people to insights about the meaning of reality, about what fosters their life together and with God. For example, people of the past came to the insight that killing others was destructive not only of the one killed but also of the killer. So they developed laws to make this insight explicit and to provide guidance.

Coming to such an insight was nothing else than the actual application of this methodology! These people recognized the basic value of life and realized that many motivations for taking life (anger, revenge and so on) did not justify this premoral evil. We know that through history some people have found reasons sufficient for taking life (self-defense, just war). Once again, these exceptions are the product of this discerning methodology. We also are aware that some people—Hitler, for example—have attempted to justify taking life, but their reasons were rejected by most people of goodwill.

MORAL NORMS

Beyond realizing that law is rooted in our method, we need one more key to understanding law. Law is expressed in different kinds of moral norms. The differences—sometimes they seem like fine distinctions—need to be appreciated so that we do not slip into an abuse or misunderstanding of the method.

Basically, moral norms reflect our two fundamental questions: "What ought I/we to do?" and "What ought I/we to be?" That is, some norms deal with actions, with our doing. These laws are called material norms. Others treat essential human characteristics, our being. These are called formal norms. As we just saw, all these norms are formulated as a result of human experience.

Continue with the example of killing: Based on experience and faith, people recognized the evil of taking another's life. A "to do" norm was therefore expressed: Do not kill. This norm is about action, about something we do. It is a norm, however, which has exceptions (at least in the judgment of many people). Some situations may justify the taking of life. We determine those exceptions by weighing the good that will be achieved (such as protecting one's own life in self-defense) against the premoral evil that will be caused (the death of an unjust aggressor). Still, the norm is generally applicable and certainly helpful in providing guidance for people's lives.

Is there a related formal norm, a norm about an essential human attitude? Yes. One way to express this norm is: Respect life. This type of norm does not describe an action but rather a quality of the truly human. It is not an optional quality or a quality that has exceptions. One must always respect life. Of course, exactly how one respects life may vary; the norm does not help us determine the specific action. Thus, it is possible to respect life (following the formal norm) and still kill someone in self-defense (making an exception to the material norm). Even though formal norms do not determine concrete actions, such norms are important in describing the truly human, in reminding us what we ought to be.

Obviously, some actions contradict material norms without a sufficient reason (killing someone out of anger). Such actions also violate the formal norm because the killer clearly shows no respect for life.

A careful understanding of these two types of norms is important for the methodology presented in this chapter. Formal norms provide insight into essential human qualities (honesty, justice, chastity, respect for life and so on). Material norms provide guidance for behavior, although exceptions are possible. Such exceptions emphasize the challenge to discern rightly the conflicting values in the concrete situation.

Some material norms, for all practical purposes, are without exception. For example, we can think of no justification for causing an infant to suffer severe pain with no benefit for the child. Given our understanding of human experience, we cannot conceive of reasons sufficient to contradict some material norms. We can regard such norms as practically absolute. But consistency in this method, humility in admitting we cannot know all situations and acceptance of being historical persons point at least to the theoretical possibility of exceptions.

One more concept deserves attention: the synthetic norm. A norm which seems to be about an action but actually also includes a moral judgment is a synthetic norm. "Do not murder" is an excellent example. Murder represents a concrete action, taking someone's life. Built into the word, however, is the judgment that there is no justifying reason for the killing. A major difference exists, then, between saying, "Do not kill" and "Do not murder." "Do not kill" relates to an action and acknowledges possible exceptions. "Do not murder" relates more to a human quality, one which would never take life in an unjustified way; it allows no exceptions.

The discerning methodology could never be used to justify murder, for the very use of the word murder includes a judgment that this action is an unjustified killing. Killing points to a reality—the taking of a life—but leaves open the question whether there exists sufficient reason for the action or not. This judgment can only be made through the discerning process described in this chapter. Recognition of this distinction keeps the methodology from being misinterpreted and points to its proper use.

Expressing the Tradition

Another concern some raise about the discerning method of making moral decisions is its relationship to the Christian tradition. Although this discussion can become very theoretical, a few major points will contribute to our appreciation of the method. For many years the principle of the double effect has provided a means for dealing with conflict situations in which a good is achieved only when some evil is caused.

Take, for example, a pregnant woman who has cancer of the uterus. The only way (for the sake of the argument) to save the mother is to remove the cancerous uterus, thereby killing the fetus. The principle of double effect requires four conditions for its application: (1) The act must be good or at least indifferent, not morally evil; (2) the intention must be the good effect of the act; (3) the evil effect cannot be the means to the good effect; (4) there must be a proportionately serious reason for tolerating the evil. In the example, the removal of the cancerous uterus was the direct means to healing the mother. The killing of the fetus was indirect and not intended.

Relying on the thought of Saint Thomas Aquinas, the proponents of the discerning method focus on the intent (2) and especially on the reason (4) rather than on the direct/indirect distinction (3). What becomes crucial for the morality of the act, then, is whether the means fulfills or contradicts the basic value, or in the language of this chapter, whether there is a sufficient reason. Our example of killing fits here: The sufficient reason of self-defense justified the taking of life, and so the act was an authentic expression of respect for life.

Another example is the difference between a falsehood and a lie. Just as killing is considered murder when there is not a sufficient reason, so telling a falsehood is considered a lie when there is not a sufficient reason, when the falsehood undermines the meaning and purpose of human speech. If an enraged person breaks into my home and demands to know the whereabouts of a friend in order to kill that friend, then I have a sufficient reason for not telling the truth. I actually protect the fundamental significance of communication by telling a falsehood.

This example leads to a related issue: the weighing or discerning of basic goods (life, freedom, justice) that seem to be in conflict. The ongoing debate about method has produced this example: A southern sheriff investigating a rape case is faced with framing a black suspect whom he knows to be innocent or carrying on a prolonged search for the real criminal while a riot threatens to break out and claim many lives.

Our discerning methodology would point out that there is no inherent connection between framing the innocent person and changing the minds of the rioting mob (unlike the earlier example in which there was an inherent connection between the death of the fetus and saving the mother's life). The mob is free to change its mind even without the framing of the innocent person; similarly, the framing will not necessarily change any minds. Therefore, framing an innocent person only seems to protect life. The manner of protecting the good (by the framing) actually undermines a related good (freedom) by supposing that the mob's choice is necessarily dependent on the sheriff's action. Because the good of life depends in part upon freedom, to undermine freedom is to undermine life. Clearly, the possibility of preventing the riot does not justify the framing of an innocent person.

In considering both the principle of double effect and the possible conflict of basic goods, the discerning method expresses a rootedness in and an appropriate contemporary articulation of the Catholic tradition in moral theology. These complex concerns also underline the challenge of this method.

MRS. BERGMEIER'S DECISION

One final example of this challenge summarizes our whole chapter: using the discerning method to evaluate Mrs. Bergmeier's moral dilemma. Rather than place the discussion in the pastor's study after her return home, let us suppose she is using the discerning method in the actual setting of the prison camp.

Mrs. Bergmeier has learned that her husband and children have been reunited and that they have been desperately trying to find her. The only way to obtain her release from prison and a return to Germany is through pregnancy. Mrs. Bergmeier faces this moral dilemma: Does she seek out someone to impregnate her so that she can return to her family or would that action contradict and undermine her commitment to her family?

Certainly Mrs. Bergmeier is faced with a profound moral dilemma, one made so much more difficult because of its setting in the fear and chaos of the prison camp. She asks: "What ought I to do?"

Mrs. Bergmeier begins her evaluation by looking carefully at the realities involved. She and her husband truly love each other; they have remained faithful to their marriage vows throughout the horrors of the war. Their love is embodied in three wonderful children. How strange, then, that this very love and commitment may lead her to seek sexual intercourse and pregnancy with someone she hardly knows. But wouldn't that price be worth paying in order to return home?

Mrs. Bergmeier continues her ponderings on the meaning of sexuality, of sexual intercourse, of marriage. Her many years of married life have taught her what a profound sharing of self and expression of love sexual intercourse is. She also knows that it is far from the totality of her relationship with her husband. Yet she wonders how he will react if she returns home pregnant.

Mrs. Bergmeier thinks about the child-to-be. What would be the meaning of the child's life? Would a baby be merely a means of escape or a symbol of her love for the family? How will the other children accept—or reject—this child? The value of family life is extremely important for Mrs. Bergmeier. She knows what her presence would mean for the children, how much they need a mother.

The guard whom she would seek out is also a concern for Mrs. Bergmeier. She asks what such an encounter would mean for him, what it would do to him. Would he merely be using the occasion for his own pleasure? Would she be using him, reducing him to a mere means of impregnation? She wonders how long it might take to become pregnant. In these many ways, Mrs. Bergmeier considers the reality of her life, the meaning of her own integrity.

As a faithful Lutheran, Mrs. Bergmeier reflects on her religious traditions and recalls passages from Scripture that she heard so often. She quietly talks to other women in the prison camp, trying to get a sense of their judgment. She even considers the particular pressures of life in the prison camp and how all that is influencing her decision. Mrs. Bergmeier bluntly asks herself: How bad must the situation be in order to justify infidelity—and would this really be infidelity?

In the end, Mrs. Bergmeier reluctantly decides that it would not be right to seek to become pregnant. She recognizes that she cannot force the freedom of those who imprison her. They may renege on the policy of releasing pregnant women. Freedom from prison may yet come from another source. Her religion gives her hope even in the face of the darkness of prison life; it reaffirms her own sense of the meaning and value of sexuality and marriage. Most important, Mrs. Bergmeier realizes that, however much she wants to be with her family, seeking to become pregnant would contradict her own integrity as a person by reducing to a mere means of escape her body, the guard and the child.

Because Mrs. Bergmeier's case is a profound dilemma and because this discerning methodology of making moral decisions is so much more nuanced than merely comparing pros and cons, sincere people may reach a different conclusion. Such a fact ought not to surprise us! Mrs. Bergmeier's case (and many of our own) is much less clear than the earlier example about amputation. In Mrs. Bergmeier's dilemma, some may judge her pregnancy as an unusual but real expression of her love and commitment to her family. The value of Mrs. Bergmeier's return is sufficient to justify the pregnancy.

Other approaches to making moral decisions might find this case less difficult to judge. Those who hold that the end justifies any means would probably easily conclude that Mrs. Bergmeier was justified in seeking out the friendly guard. Those who hold that the law provides firm guidance and demands absolute obedience would just as easily conclude that Mrs. Bergmeier violated her marriage vows and was wrong in becoming pregnant.

CONCLUDING CAUTIONS

Such diversity of judgment (along with the reminder that it might indeed be very difficult for someone in a prison camp to follow the discerning methodology in true freedom) suggests several cautions.

First, although a variety of judgments exist, realities also exist—in Mrs. Bergmeier's situation and in our own. Mrs. Bergmeier's case includes the person involved, marriage, fidelity, sexual intercourse, family life, the needs of the children, the horror of a prison camp. Some decisions more fully respect these realities and foster the development of Mrs. Bergmeier's humanity. The challenge for her (and for us in our decisions) is to discern properly these realities and to understand the implications of their meaning for our lives. The wisdom of past ages and the experience of others provide significant, if not definitive, guidance for making moral decisions. Where there is still strong disagreement about the realities and their meanings, we experience the need for various communities (academic, civil, religious) to continue the dialogue in search of more complete and satisfying understandings.

Second, the diversity of judgments reminds us that sincere people can come to different conclusions. As a result, even when we are quite confident about our judgment of a particular action, we still cannot judge the person. Such a realization does not reduce us to relativism, to a silent affirmation of whatever each person chooses. The task of ethics remains the search for truth, for understanding of reality and of what we ought to do. Yet an individual's discernment lies beyond the scope of others' knowledge. The individual's freedom—and so the possibility of a fundamental choice about life—may be limited in ways unknown to the observer. For example, we can never enter into Mrs. Bergmeier's judgments of the various realities or experience her feelings of commitment and bonding with her family or determine the influence of life in the prison camp. We can disagree with her conclusion, but we cannot judge her integrity, her relationship with God. Similarly, in the continuing and often emotional debates about such issues as abortion and euthanasia, nuclear arms and the economy, we cannot judge another individual's moral state. A profound respect for persons is required, then, even in the midst of serious disagreement about issues and actions.

Third, this mix of realities and judgments and of laws and personal decisions demonstrates the complexity and tensions involved in making moral decisions. This mix also highlights the need for a more detailed consideration of the relationship between conscience and authority—the topic of chapter three.

CATECHISM REFERENCES

Nos. 1749–1775, 1949–1986.

FOR REFLECTION AND DISCUSSION

1. This chapter described three approaches to making moral decisions: the teleological, the deontological, the discerning. Express the meaning of each of these approaches in your own words, and then give examples from your own experience of how you have used each method. What strengths and weaknesses do you find in each method?

2. What is the distinction between premoral evil and moral evil? Give some examples of premoral evil from your life.

3. Reread McCormick's six criteria for discernment (see pages 26 and 27). In *Reason Informed by Faith*, Richard Gula offers another set of questions to guide discernment of the moral dilemma: "What? Who? When? Where? Why? How? What if? What else?" Recall an important moral decision in your life. How would these questions have helped enlighten that situation?

4. Recall the difference between formal norms and material norms (see pages 29 to 30). In your own experience, how are the two kinds of norms helpful in making moral decisions? What are the limits of each? Have you ever found a material norm in conflict with a formal norm?

5. Compare this chapter's evaluation of Mrs. Bergmeier's decision with the six criteria suggested by McCormick. How does this evaluation compare with your own answer to Question 6 in chapter one? Has your position changed? Why or why not?

6. The chapter concluded with several cautions, given the diversity of moral judgments. Do you believe it possible to combine serious disagreement about an action with respect for a person? What impact would these cautions have on our nation's debates about moral issues?

chapter three

CONSCIENCE AND AUTHORITY

Making moral decisions demands mature responsibility. To seek to understand reality, to be attentive to the wisdom of the past, to discern the biases and demands of a particular situation—all of these efforts require a mature decision-maker. All of them hinge on the central role of conscience.

Conscience is a much-used—and sometimes abused—word. Accordingly, in this chapter we will take a close look at conscience and one of its most important dialogue partners, authority.

We sometimes describe conscience as a "little voice" inside our mind telling us what to do; sometimes we picture conscience as an inner police officer or as parent tapes. Such images are not satisfactory. The conscience is really the personal self as it tries to make sound judgments about our basic moral questions: "What ought I/we to be?" and "What ought I/we to do?"

Vatican II stressed both the meaning and the use of conscience. In its *Pastoral Constitution on the Church in the Modern World* (16), the Council called conscience the individual's most secret core and sanctuary where one is alone with God. There the person discovers a law inscribed by God to love, to do what is good and to avoid evil. The document states that human dignity lies in observing this law and that the person will be judged by it. Through loyalty to conscience, the Council continues, Christians are united with other people in the search for truth and for the right solution to individual and social moral problems.

Accordingly, people will want to be guided by objective standards of moral conduct. The Council adds that conscience can go astray through ignorance without losing its dignity. This is not the case, however, of the person who really does not seek to find out the true and good.

The same Council's *Declaration on Religious Liberty* added that persons, "that is, beings endowed with reason and free will and therefore bearing personal responsibility, are both impelled by their nature and bound by a moral obligation to seek the truth, especially religious truth" (2). The document points out that this search for truth must be done in a way appropriate to the human social nature, that is, by free inquiry with the help of teaching, communication and dialogue. The highest norm of life, divine law, is recognized through conscience. In order, then, to come to one's final end and fulfillment, God, the individual must follow this conscience faithfully.

THREE DIMENSIONS OF CONSCIENCE

In *Principles for a Catholic Morality*, Timothy O'Connell summarizes the tradition and presents a very concise and helpful picture of conscience, describing it as three different dimensions of a person.

The first dimension of conscience is the general sense of value that is characteristic of the human being. We are aware that we should do good and avoid evil. A sure sign of this general awareness is the fact that people argue about right and wrong. There would be no debate if we did not experience the responsibility of choosing between good and evil. Our desire to do the right thing reflects this general sense of value.

The second dimension of conscience is the search to discover the right course of action. This probing into human behavior and the world is the search for truth. If we are honest in our search, then we turn to a variety of sources for wisdom and guidance: for example, Scripture, the church, the physical and human sciences, tradition, competent professional advice.

We may often encounter conflict in this search, for we can discover a variety of interpretations of the truth. Life leads us to a number of different communities: political, social, economic, religious. These different communities all have their "experts," along with their fundamental values, meanings and messages. Our search for truth must recognize and weigh these at times competing values and meanings. Our final judgment about the moral issue facing us necessarily implies choosing which community is most significant for us, which community's values and worldview provide the basis of our own. For example, faced with a serious business dilemma, we might base our decision on the maximization of profit (influenced by the economic community) or on the value of respect for persons (influenced by the religious community).

The third dimension of conscience is the actual, concrete judgment that we make pertaining to an immediate action. After searching for the truth, we reach a point when a specific decision must be made.

Many of us have said, "I must follow my conscience." This principle is absolutely true—if it is properly understood. It also presupposes something very important: that the work of the conscience at the second dimension—

gathering the data—is fully informed. This process is also known as the formation of conscience. In other words, I must follow my decision (third dimension) only after I have done my best to search for truth concerning the issue facing me (second dimension). Following my conscience does not mean doing what I feel like doing. It does mean the work—often hard work—of discerning what is right and what is wrong.

In the example of amputating an arm, this discernment was fairly clear. Mrs. Bergmeier's situation, however, posed more challenging questions and ambiguities. Her search for truth, as we suggested in chapter two, was more complicated, more demanding. But the discerning process, the use of conscience, was fundamentally the same as in the simpler case.

As Vatican II reminded us, conscience can go astray without losing its dignity. A person could do the very best searching for the truth but still miss the mark. As a result, the decision reached might not be the one which would best lead to human fulfillment. Nonetheless, the individual must follow this decision (again, on the condition that the person really tried to discover the truth). The conscience is the individual's supreme court; its judgment must be followed.

Obviously, caution is essential here: caution on the part of the decision-maker and caution on the part of one who observes the action. The decision-maker must be careful to search for the truth of the particular issue. One can be blinded by one's own desires and so miss the realities of the situation. (*The Church in the Modern World*, especially 30 and 37, reminded us of this possibility, too.) Or one can simply be confronted with a complex situation in which the realities are difficult to discern.

The observer of the action (as we were of Mrs. Bergmeier's story) must also exercise caution. Surely the observer must search for truth and take a stand on issues. Even if the decision contradicts the one made by the decision-maker, however, the observer recognizes the impossibility of entering fully into the other's discerning process, the other's conscience. Thus the suggested evaluation of Mrs. Bergmeier's dilemma concluded that she ought not to seek to become pregnant, that her decision was the wrong decision, that there was not a sufficient reason for her infidelity. Still, we cannot judge Mrs. Bergmeier; we cannot call her morally evil. She may have done her very best in searching for the truth and may have honestly concluded that she was right in seeking out the friendly guard.

Authority

Many of the situations which confront us are also complex. That is why we cannot simply solve every issue by ourselves. We need guidance. We need to turn to Scripture and tradition and various kinds of authorities for help. This is where law and authority properly fit in the individual's discerning process, as a guide for action based on the accumulated wisdom of past generations.

Authority is another much used—and sometimes abused—word. We know that in many different situations authority has slipped into authoritarianism: using power to impose directives from the top and to demand unquestioning obedience and observance. A more positive and proper role of authority is to inspire, encourage, sensitize and lead to growth. People look to such authority for guidance and direction.

Within the Catholic church, of course, authority has a special nature and function. As the early Christian community developed, so did the need for proper authority. The community grew as a result of preaching: The disciples who had experienced the risen Jesus began to tell the story of the life, death and resurrection of Jesus, first in Jerusalem and then in other cities. Through this preaching, other people came to believe in Jesus. Communities gradually developed. The disciples moved on to new cities, leaving behind a local leader who presided at the liturgy and who was the primary teacher, faithfully yet creatively handing on the Good News.

Authority, then, plays an important and natural role in the Christian community. Through almost two thousand years of church history, many changes have occurred in the understanding and use of authority. We recognize not only the historical conditioning of these changes but also their strengths and weaknesses. In the contemporary Catholic church, authority continues to be discussed—and often misunderstood, especially regarding the topic of infallibility. Correcting these misunderstandings will lead us not only to an appropriate appreciation of authority but also to a better sense of the relationship between authority and conscience.

The Catholic church holds that the pope and the bishops in union with the pope enjoy teaching prerogatives of a unique kind. The pope and bishops are commissioned to teach authoritatively on faith and morals in a way no other teacher in the church can claim to do. Catholic teaching holds that the supreme doctrinal authority in the Roman Catholic church is all the bishops together with and under the pope. In the contemporary church this teaching authority is called the *magisterium*. The guidance and pastoral concern of this teaching authority is a great gift to the church. Aided by the Holy Spirit, the magisterium helps protect the church from needless errors and wrong turns.

The word *magisterium* itself causes some confusion. Only in recent history has the word been so exclusively linked to the pope and other bishops. From the Latin word meaning "teacher," *magisterium* has also been used to describe theologians and other teachers. Some people still wish to use the word that way today, although such use may contribute to the confusion. Another way to respect the various gifts and responsibilities of different groups (especially bishops and theologians) and at the same time to reduce confusion is simply to clarify the full meaning of *magisterium* when applied to the pope and other bishops. This clarification includes the precise consideration of these related topics: collegiality, infallibility, non-infallible teachings, the official teachers as learners and the relation to conscience.

COLLEGIALITY

In its discussion of church authority, Vatican II stressed that all the bishops (the college of bishops) share responsibility for the church, not just the pope. The pope, however, is head of this college. Therefore, even when he acts separately (that is, not specifically commissioned by the rest of the bishops), he acts as the visible head of the church—and indeed as head of the college of bishops. The concepts of "pope" and "college of bishops" are inseparable from each other. There is one supreme authority which can be expressed in two ways: (1) through a collegiate act (as in an ecumenical council, a worldwide gathering of bishops) or (2) through the act of the pope as head of the college (as in an encyclical letter).

Another distinction applies to these two expressions of the supreme teaching authority: the distinction between extraordinary and ordinary magisterium. The teaching authority is called "extraordinary" when it refers to a solemn act of defining a dogma of faith—that is, an infallible pronouncement of some truth as divinely revealed for the sake of our salvation. In this context, *define* means giving a definitive judgment on a particular question. Either an ecumenical council or a pope can exercise extraordinary teaching authority. The most recent example of such a pronouncement is the teaching about the Assumption of Mary, which was defined by Pope Pius XII in 1950.

Any other exercise of the teaching authority of the bishops or the pope is called "ordinary." Examples of this ordinary teaching authority include the teachings of a local bishop, the pastoral letters of the bishops' conference, the encyclical letters of the popes and the documents of Vatican II (because the Council did not use its authority to define any new dogma of Catholic faith). Although these teachings are certainly authoritative, they do not as such fall under the category of infallible teaching.

At the risk of confusion—but actually for the sake of clarity—one more point must be made: The universal ordinary magisterium—that is, the teaching of all the bishops dispersed throughout the world with the pope—can proclaim doctrine infallibly. In other words, there can be cases of infallible teaching by ordinary magisterium. Examples of such teachings not solemnly defined but taught as divinely revealed include some of the basic articles of the Christian faith: for example, that Jesus is Lord and that God raised him from the dead.

INFALLIBILITY

But what is infallibility? The heart of infallibility is this: The power of divine grace (not the human strength of its members) cannot allow the church as a whole to fall away from the truth of God. Simply put, the presence of God will not allow the church to self-destruct. Infallibility is a characteristic of the church, vested in those who have supreme authority over the whole church. As stated above, this supreme authority is the college of bishops with the pope as its head.

Infallibility, thus, is not a characteristic of the pope's personal conduct or his private views. Even when Vatican I (1869–1870) defined papal infallibility, it did so in terms of the church. Vatican I stated that when the pope defines a dogma of faith (often described as speaking *ex cathedra*— "from the chair") he is gifted by the Holy Spirit with that infallibility God desired for the church in defining a doctrine of faith or morals.

Vatican II reemphasized this point:

> This infallibility, however, with which the divine redeemer
> wished to endow his church in defining doctrine pertaining
> to faith and morals, extends just as far as the deposit of reve-

lation, which must be religiously guarded and faithfully expounded. The Roman Pontiff, head of the college of bishops, enjoys this infallibility in virtue of his office, when, as supreme pastor and teacher of all the faithful—who confirms his brothers and sisters in the faith (see Luke 22:32)—he proclaims in a definitive act a doctrine pertaining to faith or morals....The infallibility promised to the church is also present in the body of bishops when, together with Peter's successor, they exercise the supreme teaching office. (*Dogmatic Constitution on the Church*, 25)

Infallibility does not mean that the church will never make mistakes. The church has certainly made its share: for example, in science, the Galileo case; in human rights, the practice of slavery. History reveals many other mistakes. Infallibility does mean that the church is not going to self-destruct because the presence of the Spirit at work in the community will prevent this. This conviction, of course, cannot be proved; it is a statement of faith. This conviction, rooted in the experience of the church and expressed in the Scriptures in Jesus' promise to be with his followers, is validated again and again throughout the centuries in the life of the Christian community. The presence and action of the Spirit will not allow the church as a whole to turn away from God!

Two modern councils—Vatican I and Vatican II—specified the conditions necessary for an expression of an infallible doctrinal pronouncement. Conditions for such a pronouncement are: (1) It must be a collegial act dealing with a revealed truth concerning faith or morals; (2) there must be an explicit call for absolute assent; (3) the pronouncement must be the unanimous teaching of all the bishops. Thus, infallibility means that the Holy Spirit so assists the magisterium that it solemnly obliges the faithful to believe only what is contained in God's word. Vatican II's *Constitution on Divine Revelation* describes the magisterium's role this way:

...[T]he task of giving an authentic interpretation of the word of God, whether in its written form or in the form of tradition, has been entrusted to the living teaching office of the church alone. Its authority in this matter is exercised in the name of Jesus Christ. This magisterium is not superior to the word of God, but is rather its servant. It teaches only what has been handed on to it. At the divine command and with the help of the Holy Spirit, it listens to this devoutly, guards it reverently and expounds it faithfully. All that it proposes for belief as being divinely revealed it draws from this sole deposit of faith. (10)

Infallibility guarantees the truth of the meaning of a statement, not the particular formulation of the meaning. As times and cultures change, particular words, concepts or theological viewpoints may need to change in order to express their central meaning. Given these severely limiting conditions for an infallible pronouncement, they are very rare. Indeed, in the twentieth century there was only one: the definition of Mary's Assumption (1950).

NON-INFALLIBLE TEACHINGS

What, then, is to be said about other official statements—such as the documents of Vatican II and papal encyclicals? Not too creatively, these documents are called non-infallible but authoritative teachings. They are not infallible declarations, yet they carry the weight of the magisterium. A proper understanding of non-infallible, authoritative teachings is absolutely essential for clarifying the confusion surrounding infallibility.

Non-infallible, authoritative teachings of the church are presumed to be true. This presumption is based on the faith-conviction that the Spirit is present in the magisterium, guiding it so that its teaching will be accurate. When an official teaching is given, the theoretically expected response of the Roman Catholic is: "This is a true teaching."

Still, non-infallible teachings do not require blind acceptance. To respond to such a teaching with the religious submission of will and of mind called for at Vatican II necessarily includes study, discussion, reflection and prayer. Such a response takes seriously the distinction between infallible and non-infallible teachings. Such a response also steers between two extremes: (1) an absolute, blind submission to authority (an approach which seems to say that the reasons for the teaching really do not matter) and (2) the rejection of any unique teaching prerogative on the part of the magisterium (an approach which judges the argument to be only as good as the reasons given). The proper response finds a delicate blend of individual reflection and of acceptance of the authoritative role of the magisterium.

Such a response also acknowledges—and here is where caution is especially needed—the possibility of error. Non-infallible teachings can miss the mark, as Vatican II demonstrated in revising earlier teachings regarding religious freedom, for example. This is part of the distinction between infallible and non-infallible teachings. If the magisterium is carefully doing its preparation for such non-infallible teachings, however, then such occasions of error should be very rare. To sum up then, even in non-infallible yet authoritative teachings, the presupposition of truth is in favor of the teaching.

This is not to say that people may never genuinely question such non-infallible teachings. Such questioning occurred very publicly in the debate over artificial contraception. At other times, the debate has centered on the church's teaching about politics, economics and other social justice issues. For example, Paul VI's encyclical on the development of peoples was dismissed by some as warmed-over Marxism.

Not all of these controversies result merely from the casual rejection of the magisterium's authority. At the root of this debate and division, some scholars state, is an inconsistency in the way judgments about morality are made. Church teachings seem to be reached by using two different methods for making judgments. One way, the classicist or physicalist approach, emphasizes abstract principles, biology and the answers of tradition, and then stresses the need to obey these answers. Many of the teachings on sexuality and medical issues are arrived at by this method.

The second way, the modern or personalist method, is quite different. It starts with an understanding of the human being which is based on the key ideas and images of the Bible. It also emphasizes the need to be open to input from contemporary sciences and calls for personal and communal responsibility. Many of the social teachings are arrived at by this method. This method better embodies Vatican II's directive that all dimensions of well-being be included in judging the morality of human action.

A Crisis of Credibility

In her 1989 John Courtney Murray Forum Lecture, Margaret O'Brien Steinfels names the situation of doubt and debate in the church a "crisis of plausibility."

She clearly articulates what many others have said and even more have experienced: that in the contemporary church there is a crisis of credibility. The crisis, she judges, is symbolized by the use of language because words are used to veil intentions rather than to disclose realities. Steinfels cites "collegiality" as an example, stating: "It is now used mostly by people who by their actions have just demonstrated that it doesn't mean anything."

The result is that some people cease to believe the official version of anything, but instead believe the opposite. Others end up believing nothing. Steinfels notes that:

> Too often the language Catholics hear coming from the Vatican seems to have no real resonance in their lives. Too often our church leaders deftly avoid a whole range of realities that are deemed taboo or futile for discussion. Too often Catholics, lay and clergy, end by assuming the worst and seizing upon the very opposite of the official version. Or they fill up the hole left by their skepticism with new shibboleths.

Steinfels sees authority as one factor of this crisis of credibility. (The other two factors she describes are gender and the relationship of church and world.) Vatican II's emphasis on collegiality and the priesthood of all the baptized led to new structures of authority and community. More traditional models were not abandoned, but synods, senates and councils appeared, all emphasizing collaboration and service.

Such an understanding and implementation of authority fit contemporary experience, in which one acquires authority through competence, commitment, character and courage. Steinfels names Dorothy Day, Karl Rahner and Oscar Romero as examples of people whose authority continues even after death. The more structured form of authority, acquired by virtue of role or office, of course also continued to exist.

Crisis emerges when the spirit of authority does not match changes in structure. As a result, Steinfels finds greater gaps between words and deeds. "National episcopal conferences are under attack. Bishops are sworn to hold a certain line. Calls are heard for uniformity and obedience....The principles of participation and subsidiarity notwithstanding, the pressures for centralization of authority in the church grow apace." Authority is actually undermined rather than restored when people claim more authority than the circumstances warrant. Here Steinfels blames both theologians and the Vatican.

Such a crisis clearly calls for a response from the whole church: the magisterium and the whole people of God. It is the responsibility of the magisterium, like every good teacher, carefully to do its homework. Being official teachers demands being official learners as well. The Spirit's presence that guides the magisterium is a gift. But the Spirit is present in other people and events also! The magisterium must therefore make every effort to listen and to learn from as many sources as possible: not only Scripture and tradition, but also theologians, psychologists, sociologists, physicians and just plain people.

Just as the church holds that the Spirit infallibly guides the magisterium so that it does not propose teachings that would lead the whole church into error, so it also holds that the faithful, as a whole, have an instinct or "sense" about when a teaching is—or is not—in harmony with the true faith. This special *sensus fidelium*, "consensus of the faithful," is one of the ways the Spirit protects God's people from error.

Vatican II described this aspect of the church when it taught: "The whole body of the faithful who have received an anointing which comes from the holy one (see 1 John 2:20, 27) cannot be mistaken in belief. It shows this characteristic through the entire people's supernatural sense of the faith, when, 'from the bishops to the last of the faithful,' it manifests a universal consensus in matters of faith and morals" (*Dogmatic Constitution on the Church*, 12).

Such openness acknowledges that the Spirit is teaching in the experience of experts and of ordinary folks alike. Vatican II expressed this conviction well in *The Church in the Modern World*:

> Indeed, this kind of adaptation and preaching of the revealed Word must ever be the law of all evangelization....Nowadays when things change so rapidly and thought patterns differ so widely, the Church needs to step up this exchange by calling upon the help of people who are living in the world, who are expert in its organizations and its forms of training, and who understand its mentality, in the case of believers and non-believers alike. With the help of the Holy Spirit, it is the task of the whole people of God, particularly of its pastors and

theologians, to listen to and distinguish the many voices of our times and to interpret them in the light of the divine Word, in order that the revealed truth may be more deeply penetrated, better understood, and more suitably presented. (44)

Theologians and others with special competence also have a responsibility to deal with the crisis of credibility both by their ongoing research and, if necessary, by their disagreement. Sometimes, discussion and dissent are interpreted in purely negative ways, seen as the hostile rejection of authority. Because most of the magisterium's teachings fall under the non-infallible category, however, error is possible. Respectful dissent, properly expressed, in the long run can help refine and enrich the teaching. Discussion and disagreement may help ensure that official teaching will not be expressed in incomplete or erroneous ways. Indeed, such dissent may be necessary for the health of the church.

In their pastoral letter *Human Life in Our Day*, the bishops of the United States discussed norms of licit dissent: "The expression of theological dissent from the magisterium is in order only if the reasons are serious and well-founded, if the manner of the dissent does not question or impugn the teaching authority of the Church and is such as not to give scandal" (51). The bishops recognize theologians' distinct gifts and responsibilities, but they remind the professionals that not everyone has the same special competence. Accordingly, theologians must be sensitive in how they express their views, also remembering the presumption in favor of the magisterium.

THE CRISIS CONTINUES

Several years after the Steinfels lecture, disagreement and discussion came from surprising sources, powerfully symbolizing the continuation of the crisis. First, John Quinn, the then recently retired archbishop of San Francisco, called for the restructuring of the Roman Curia and other changes. Second, Cardinal Joseph Bernardin of Chicago announced the Catholic Common Ground Project, an effort to overcome polarization in the church. Both events evoked a wide range of reactions.

Archbishop Quinn was responding to an invitation issued by Pope John Paul II in his 1995 encyclical on ecumenism. The pope asked for public consideration of how the papacy can be embodied and exercised in the "new situation" of today's world. In his carefully argued and documented address, Archbishop Quinn called for greater pastoral sensitivity in exercising the church's ministry. He stressed the importance of major structural reform of the congregations, secretariats and tribunals that make up the Curia. Quinn was concerned both with specific issues (such as the appointment of bishops, the approval of documents such as the *Catechism*, celibacy, the role of conferences of bishops, the ordination of women) and with the way decisions about these issues are made. This reform would be studied and directed by a three-member commission, one of whom would be a layperson, assisted by a larger commission of bishops, priests, religious and laypeople.

Quinn urged a number of other changes: (1) giving local churches a more significant role in the appointment of bishops; (2) paying greater appreciation to subsidiarity (letting more local bodies fulfill their own functions, for example, a diocese or bishops' conference instead of the Vatican); (3) creating a more open atmosphere for bishops themselves to discuss the debated issues, and so embody and express collegiality—a fundamental topic in Quinn's lecture; (4) gathering more frequently as church in ecumenical councils, including one to mark the beginning of the millennium.

In announcing the Catholic Common Ground Project, Cardinal Bernardin described how the crisis has spread to all parts of the church: "I have been troubled that an increasing polarization within the church and, at times, a mean-spiritedness have hindered the kind of dialogue that helps us address our mission and concerns." He added, "The unity of the church is threatened, the great gift of the Second Vatican Council is in danger of being seriously undermined, the faithful members of the church are weary, and our witness to government, society and culture is compromised." The purpose of the project, expressed in the document *Called to Be Catholic: Church in a Time of Peril*, was to bring people together for dialogue leading to mutual understanding. Some of the specific problems that the project intended to address included ineffective religious education, the changing roles of women, dissent over church teachings on sexuality and, especially, the underlying mood of suspicion and bitterness. Reactions both from other cardinals and from liberal and conservative groups only seemed to underline the separation, fear and suspicion within the church. Shortly before he died in 1996, Cardinal Bernardin said that the criticisms reflected the church's "current state of nervous anxiety." He stressed that the project would not compromise the truth of Catholic doctrine but would be accountable to Scripture, tradition and church teaching. Indeed, the project's goal "is the fullest possible understanding of and internalization of the truth."

THE CRISIS INTENSIFIES

The church's crisis of credibility exploded in a dramatic new way in 2002. Revelations of sexual abuse by clergy, already in the news for years, now included more direct charges of cover-ups of those crimes by bishops. Articles in the *Boston Globe* about Cardinal Law and former priest John Geoghan started an avalanche of accusations, reactions, studies, and stories of survivors. (See "Ethics and the Crisis in the Church" by James Keenan, S.J., for an extensive bibliography.)

Many commentators reflected not only on the horror of the abuse but also on the damage done to the integrity of the priesthood and the credibility of the bishops. The April 1, 2002, editorial from *America*, "Healing and Credibility," gives an accurate sense of the situation, describing it as "a crisis that is causing enormous pain and great scandal in the church." The editorial affirms that the crimes of sexual abuse "have physically, psychologically and spiritually damaged hundreds, perhaps thousands, of children and their families." And it adds that the "attempts by some bishops to cover up the crimes have shocked those in and outside the church more than any other event in memory. The fact that abusive priests were reassigned to other parishes, where they again violated children, is deplorable and inexcusable."

Similar judgments were expressed by many others, including Michael Sean Winters. He writes: "Multimillion-dollar payouts to victims don't threaten the church nearly as much as does the further loss of confidence in the moral compass of its bishops."

Facing growing anger, pressure and hostility from victims, media and members of the church, the U.S. bishops attempted to answer the fundamental question: What can be done to protect children and restore the credibility of the church? In their June 2002 meeting in Dallas, the bishops approved the *Charter for the Protection of Children and Young People* along with the "Essential Norms" necessary for implementing the policies of the charter. These texts were slightly revised after consultation with Vatican officials and approved by the bishops in their November 2002 meeting.

A key point in the charter is "zero tolerance." Any priest who has abused a minor would not be allowed to function as a priest again, even if there had been only one incident years in the past. This point was debated by the bishops, especially in light of the bishops' conference's critique of the United States criminal justice system's emphasis on harsh sentences. Nevertheless, in an attempt to restore trust, the majority of the bishops accepted the zero-tolerance policy.

Another major decision in the charter is not to require forced laicization of all sexual abusers. Reasons for this choice included the desire not to treat retired or infirm priests cruelly and the recognition that keeping the priest under some kind of supervision would better protect children.

The charter also creates accountability procedures and committees, with significant emphasis on lay leadership. The Office of Child and Youth Protection offers assistance to safe environment programs run by dioceses and to victims' assistance coordinators. It has also developed a report on the implementation of the charter. This 2004 report found that most of the dioceses were implementing the charter.

The charter also established the National Review Board. This board reviews and approves the implementation report and has commissioned its own study. This John Jay study reviews sexual abuse information in the dioceses from 1950 to 2002, reporting that there were more than four thousand priests accused and more than ten thousand victims.

The charter does not punish the bishops who simply transferred priest-abusers to a different parish. In his address at the meeting, Bishop Wilton Gregory, then president of the bishops' conference, did call for confession and contrition and apologized to victims and their families. He acknowledged that the crisis is about the profound loss of confidence by the members of the church in the bishops.

In opening the session, Bishop Gregory said that the bishops need to confess:

> We are the ones, whether through ignorance or lack of vigilance, or, God forbid, with knowledge, who allowed priest abusers to remain in ministry and reassigned them to communities where they continued to abuse.

We are the ones who chose not to report the criminal actions of priests to the authorities because the law did not require this.

We are the ones who worried more about the possibility of scandal than in bringing about the kind of openness that helps prevent abuse. And we are the ones who, at times, responded to victims and their families as adversaries and not as suffering members of the church.

After the dust of the Dallas meeting settled, questions emerged—questions about due process, the definition of sexual abuse, the burden of proof, statutes of limitations, the rights of accused priests. In "Rights of Accused Priests," Cardinal Avery Dulles, S.J., has rather bluntly addressed these and other concerns. Before a brief reflection on each topic, Cardinal Dulles strongly critiques the Dallas charter: "The bishops adopted the very principles that they themselves had condemned in their critique of the secular judicial system. In so doing they undermined the morale of their priests and inflicted a serious blow to the credibility of the church as a mirror of justice."

Other convictions, of course, continue to be expressed, especially by groups representing victims. Full disclosure and resignation of bishops are frequent demands from such groups. Others work for transformation of church structures of governance, emphasizing transparency, accountability and lay involvement. One initiative that has grown out of the crisis is Voice of the Faithful, a lay organization that has spread quickly. This group of committed Roman Catholics especially promotes greater lay participation in the governance of the church.

Not surprisingly, surveys affirm many of the themes of this new crisis. While U.S. Catholics remain committed to the church, they express overwhelming disapproval of the bishops' handling of the sexual abuse crisis. Surveys also indicate Catholics desire greater accountability by the bishops and greater participation by the laity in providing direction for the church. While some Catholics are giving less money to the church, they are not leaving the church because of the scandal.

Just before the Dallas meeting, John R. Quinn, the retired archbishop of San Francisco, wrote another very reflective essay: "Considerations for a

Church in Crisis." His counsel is straightforward: "The church must address the deeper questions. A superficial response will not do." Along with the need for a nationally binding policy for dealing with sexual abuse, Archbishop Quinn describes the deeper issues: recognition of the worldwide problems in the area of sexuality, the meaningful implementation of episcopal collegiality, and the need for strong lay involvement.

At present, trials and settlements drag on. New revelations and accusations stir up bitter emotions. Questions and doubts about revising the norms and implementing them in the long haul continue. Some of the deeper issues are not being addressed. The crisis of credibility intensifies; restoring trust once lost is not easy.

CONSCIENCE AND RESPONSIBILITY

As the crisis of credibility spreads throughout the church, it confronts all the people of God. They may not have the same gifts and responsibilities as the official teachers or the special competence of the theologians, but they have freedom, and theirs is the basic responsibility of making moral decisions. They face the continuing challenge of forming and using their conscience. Even more, as Vatican II reminded us, because of their life in the world and because of their own expertise, the people of God play a special role in the search for truth and for better understanding and better expression of revelation.

Authority and the individual self meet in conscience, then—specifically in the second dimension of conscience—as the person searches for the truth of the moral dilemma. This search involves reflection upon basic sources of information in the church: Scripture and tradition. It includes the wisdom of the ages as expressed in law. It looks for contemporary insights from sciences of all kinds. It takes personal experience seriously. Official church teaching (including non-infallible, authoritative statements) has a privileged role here.

Catholics are to take non-infallible church teachings very seriously in forming their consciences. As indicated earlier, non-infallible church teaching is expressed in different forms: in papal letters and council documents, also in local letters and directives, such as the American bishops' pastoral letters on war and peace and on the economy. These latter statements do not claim to have the same weight as the documents of Vatican II. Yet they do represent the collective teaching of the bishops of the United States. Accordingly, individuals must take this teaching seriously in the formation of conscience.

A proper understanding of non-infallible church teaching and of conscience focuses attention on mature, personal responsibility in making moral decisions. Some of us grew up in a church that so stressed the importance of authority that blind obedience became the expected response. We were not helped to form mature consciences, nor were we encouraged to accept the burden of personal responsibility described in these chapters. Yet such responsibility is an essential dimension of mature morality. We are not robots merely to be programmed in order to act. As human beings created in God's image, we have the right and responsibility to experience, to reflect, to pray and to decide.

To say that, of course, does not make it easy to do. Automatically following a teaching or law can protect us from personal responsibility and involvement; it can become merely a security blanket. On the other hand, making a mature conscience decision that conflicts with a given teaching can cause guilt feelings. Reading a book will change little of that. Only gradually can we develop not only the process of making mature moral decisions but also the ability to live in peace with those decisions.

The previous paragraph was addressed especially to those whose true freedom has been limited by excessive emphasis on the "letter of the law." The identical response, however, is just as applicable to those who act exactly opposite—those for whom law and official teachings mean little or nothing. How many people simply do not know or have ignored the official teachings! To these people, too, is addressed the challenge of making mature moral judgments—and not merely doing something because one wants to do it or because society promotes it. These people, too, must accept the burden of searching for truth, of listening to the wisdom of authority and the guidance of its teaching, of pondering their own experience in an unselfish openness to God.

The discerning method of decision-making, which recognizes the privileged guidance of the magisterium and the sanctity of conscience, rejects the extremes of blind obedience and relativism. It accepts the demands of an intelligent, informed, mature morality.

SOME FINAL WORDS

A lengthy quotation from Karl Rahner summarizes well the topics of this chapter. Rahner, who suffered the horrors of Hitler's Germany and the Communist domination of Eastern Europe, is well known as a person who loved the church. He had a profound grasp of and respect for the Christian tradition and desired to find appropriate ways to express that tradition in the contemporary world. In 1959, several years before Vatican II, Rahner wrote:

> The people in the church...must be brought up in a responsible spirit of obedience and be able to make proper use of their right to express their opinions. They must learn that this right to express their own views and to criticize others does not mean license to indulge in savage attacks and arrogant presumption. They must be brought up in a proper critical spirit toward church matters....They must learn to unite the inevitable detachment of a critical public attitude with a genuine and inspired love of the church and a genuine subordination and submission to the actual official representatives of the church. They must learn that even in the church there can be a body something like Her Majesty's Opposition, which in the course of church history has always had its own kind of saints in its ranks—the ranks of a genuine, divinely-willed opposition to all that is merely human in the church and her official representatives.
>
> They must learn—and this is not just a matter of course, but means a serious effort of education—that there are circumstances in which people can have a real duty to speak their minds within the permitted limits and in a proper spirit of respect, even though this will not bring them praise and gratitude "from above" (how many examples there are of this in the history of the saints!)....Ultimately, no formal rule can be laid down as to how to achieve a concrete synthesis of what are apparently...opposing virtues. It will come about only when people truly seek, not their own will and opinions and self-justification, but the will of God and the church— ultimately, in fact, when people are saints.
>
> We are living during a period of transition, which means, so far as our present question is concerned, at a time when certain outward forms, which have so far been useful or at

least have existed for a long time are now proving themselves less useful and effective in promoting church authority.... Apart from anything else, the church today should be more careful than ever before not to give even the slightest impression that she is of the same order as those totalitarian states for whom outward power and sterile, silent obedience are everything and love and freedom nothing, and that her methods of government are those of the totalitarian systems in which public opinion has become a Ministry of Propaganda. But we—both those of us who are in authority and those who are under authority—are perhaps still accustomed here and there to certain patriarchal forms of leadership and obedience which have no essential or lasting connection with the real stuff of church authority and obedience. (*Free Speech in the Church*)

With Rahner's words of wisdom, we conclude our study of the fundamental building blocks of contemporary Catholic morality. For the rest of this book we will turn to a number of urgent moral concerns.

CATECHISM REFERENCES
Nos. 1776–1802, 2030–2051, 2389.

FOR REFLECTION AND DISCUSSION
1. Reflect on situations in your life in which conscience played a major role. How did you know when you had adequately completed your search for truth? Has this chapter changed your understanding of conscience?
2. Compare a gospel view with an advertising slogan. How do these different worldviews influence your process of making moral decisions? How do you choose your fundamental values? What are they? How can you share with others your gospel values?
3. In *Principles for a Catholic Morality,* Timothy O'Connell wrote: "To be moral persons they must maximize the goods and minimize the evils. For only in that way can they fulfill themselves and their world. If they are sincere, then their life as a religious enterprise is safeguarded. But for moral persons, pre-

cisely because they are sincere, sincerity is not enough. They yearn also to be correct. And this not in order to be self-righteous but that good may truly flourish...." How do you react to this quotation? What relationship do you see between O'Connell's sincerity and correctness and this chapter's emphasis on following one's conscience and searching for the truth?

4. What has been your experience of authority in the church? What is needed for authority to be credible? Reflect on this chapter's description of infallibility. How does this compare with your previous understanding?

5. What attitudes and values are expressed by your own responses to non-infallible, authoritative teachings of the church? Do you find the "delicate blend" both of individual reflection and of acceptance of the proper role of the magisterium possible? How can dissent be harmful? How can it be helpful?

6. How has the abuse scandal impacted you and your family? Your parish and diocese? What steps ought the church take in order to rebuild trust?

7. How are Rahner's thoughts, expressed before Vatican II, appropriate for our day? What concretely do they imply for your life?

part two

CONTEMPORARY MORAL ISSUES

Three sexual issues that have caused much tension between conscience and authority are homosexuality, abortion and birth control. The tensions represent very different struggles. The experience and practice of many people differ from the official birth control teaching expressed in the 1968 encyclical *Humanae Vitae* (*On Human Life*) and other writings of the popes and bishops. While discussion about abortion increases within the church, the greater struggle has been with civil authority and the law of the land. Homosexuality combines both of these struggles. In this chapter, we will reflect upon these three issues, important in themselves, as examples of the relationship among conscience, authority and non-infallible teachings.

HOMOSEXUALITY

Is raising questions about our beliefs and morals a threat to our relationship with God or to life in the church? Vatican II did not think so! Instead, following Pope John XXIII's lead, the Council saw new questions as an opportunity for "a more precise and deeper understanding of [the] faith . . . . For the deposit and the truths of faith are one thing; the manner of expressing them is quite another" (*Church in the Modern World,* 62).

Search for Truth

Human beings necessarily live in and are influenced by a particular time and place and culture; no one can stand outside of history. Every human expression is limited to particular concepts and perspectives. "Limited," of course, does not mean untrue, but is a reminder that no one possesses complete objectivity and all understanding.

In the same way, church teachings and even Scripture are limited. It simply cannot be otherwise. We can discover truth, but along the way we may find clearer ways to express it. That is what Vatican II is affirming.

In their introduction to Karl Rahner's *The Practice of Faith*, Bishop Karl Lehmann and Albert Raffelt have expressed a similar insight: "God's response never fails to transcend our capacity to ask questions, and the spiritually alert Christian, indeed the human being as human being, must continue to swing the hard, sober hammer of inquiry. There are no forbidden questions, then, nor any false pride in some inviolable, final 'possession' of understanding."

Simply stated, we must always ask questions. We must not grow complacent with given answers. We must search to see truth more clearly. All this means hard work!

Why is this insight so important? Because we are tempted to stop too soon in our search for the truth about meaning and morality in our lives. We may be tempted just to follow our private feelings and good intentions, and so fail to consult the wisdom sources of church and society. Relativism results from this emphasis on the individual.

On the other hand, we are tempted to merely accept past answers and explanations, even when there are valid reasons for questioning those answers. In fact, many people were raised to respond with this almost blind obedience; some in the church today would still have us act that way.

Either response, however, as indicated in the quotations above, would undermine who we are as Christians and as human beings. We would short-circuit the search for truth.

Questions and Debate

The issue of homosexuality is a perfect example. In recent years in our society, this topic has produced much emotion, rhetoric and reaction. There is also sincere, committed experience and serious scholarship, though often leading to conflicting conclusions. Recently, the debate has spilled over into the question of same-sex marriages.

This section can only briefly consider the teaching and scholarship on homosexuality. Catholic teaching is clear, as summarized in the *Catechism* and in the U.S. bishops' *Always Our Children: A Pastoral Message to Parents of Homosexual Children and Suggestions for Pastoral Ministers*.

The bishops' statement seeks to offer pastoral guidance, and so only summarizes key aspects of the church's teaching as a foundation for its comments. Central to this teaching is the distinction between homosexual orientation and homosexual behavior. Homosexual orientation, the emotional and sexual attraction toward individuals of the same sex, is generally experienced as a given and not as something freely chosen—and so is not an issue of morality. Many experts conclude that genetic, hormonal and psychological factors lead to this orientation.

Homosexual behavior is judged objectively immoral because it contradicts the meaning of sexual intercourse. The bishops restate the Catholic tradition that "only within marriage does sexual intercourse fully symbolize the Creator's dual design, as an act of covenant love, with the potential of cocreating new human life." Genital sexual expression is to be unitive and procreative, love-giving and life-giving.

Other important points in the statement include: (1) an emphasis on the whole person; total personhood is more than just one's sexuality; (2) everyone is created in God's image, and so has inherent dignity; (3) all forms of discrimination, from humor to violence, must be stopped; nothing "in the Bible or in Catholic teaching can be used to justify prejudicial or discriminatory attitudes and behaviors"; (4) sensitivity to the range of feelings of parents, encouragement to love and support homosexual children, a list of pastoral recommendations for families and church ministers.

Scripture and the more philosophical understanding of human nature (natural law) are generally given as the foundations of this teaching. Serious debate has now developed about these foundations.

It is helpful to recall that the Bible has only five main references to homosexuality: Leviticus 18:22 and 20:13, 1 Corinthians 6:9, 1 Timothy 1:10, Romans 1:26–27. (The story of Sodom in Genesis 19:1–25 is about doing violence to strangers. The prophet Ezekiel in 16:49 actually describes Sodom's sin this way: Sodom "had pride, excess of food, and prosperous ease, but did not aid the poor and needy.") The four Gospels never describe Jesus addressing the topic of homosexuality.

Interpretation of the passages leads to the debate. Some scholars see them clearly forbidding homosexual activity (for example, Cardinal Ratzinger's 1986 letter *The Pastoral Care of Homosexual Persons*). Others claim that none of the passages is discussing the reality we understand today, for homosexual orientation was not recognized until the nineteenth century. The biblical writers had no concept or understanding of this reality and the possibility of faithful, committed, same-sex relationships. Instead, the biblical authors were concerned about purity laws, reproductive potential or persons acting sexually in dominating or passive ways (and so confusing what was thought to be "natural"), including such situations as pederasty, prostitution and humiliation of others.

Similar disagreement arises when discussing the other foundation of the church's teaching, natural law. Especially since *Humanae Vitae* (the birth control encyclical) there has been a debate within Catholic moral theology about two different methods of interpreting human nature, one with more emphasis on biology and the other on the whole person. These two views often lead to different judgments about the morality of human acts, especially sexual ones.

The experiences of homosexual persons also call for respectful consideration. These experiences include relationships of commitment and love, but also stigma and prejudice and even violence at the hands of persons and institutions.

A Possible Next Step

These questions about the foundations of the church's teaching and these challenging human experiences of good and evil suggest that now might be a good time to review carefully the teaching on homosexuality. Being clear and long-lasting does not always mean that a teaching is completely accurate. (Recall, for example, the church's long support of slavery that was based on biblical reasons.)

Such evaluation might lead to change or to reaffirmation. It would allow for more confidence in the final position. Merely repeating a teaching that has been seriously and respectfully questioned does not lead to the same kind of confidence.

How could this review happen? In an open and honest search for the truth, the church could gather experts of various disciplines and perspectives along with people of different orientations sharing their experiences of life-giving and love-giving commitments. In the context of trust in the Spirit's guidance, this board would address questions about the tradition's understanding of homosexual actions, questions rooted in contemporary understanding of Scripture, in the recognition of deep-seated prejudice, and in careful attention to people's experience.

Swinging "the hard, sober hammer of inquiry" requires openness yet faithfulness, recognition of the possibility of mistakes yet the willingness to risk. Questions do not necessarily lead to change. But we must ask the questions so that the church does not get stuck in incomplete or even wrong teaching. In our tradition's history, happily, people did ask questions about the church's positions on slavery, on economics, on the death penalty. In these areas, questions did lead to change, to a "more precise and deeper understanding" of truth.

ABORTION

Abortion confronts us both as an urgent moral issue and as a difficult legal one. Indeed, the issue of abortion focuses our attention on the distinction between morality and legality. The two themes often merge, but we also need to remember the distinction between what is moral and what is legal.

The Moral Issue

Let's begin with morality. In its official teachings, the church has expressed its position in very strong language. *The Church in the Modern World* stated: "Life must be protected with the utmost care from the moment of conception: abortion and infanticide are abominable crimes" (51). In their pastoral letter on the moral life, *To Live in Christ Jesus*, the bishops of the United States said: "To destroy these innocent unborn children is an unspeakable crime, a crime which subordinates weaker members of the human community to the interests of the stronger."

This strong position is rooted in the church's conviction that human life begins at conception and in its understanding of and emphasis on human dignity. In chapter one we reviewed the Christian tradition's understanding of the human being: Created in God's image, redeemed by Jesus and called to the fullness of life, every human being has a unique value and dignity. The word *person* is especially problematic in the abortion debate. (People often define "person" in a way that either assures certain rights or denies them to this new being.) Nevertheless, it is clear that human life begins at fertilization. What comes from fertilization is a new reality: living, not dead; human, not any other kind of being. All that is needed is the proper environment to develop. This human life has value and dignity and so deserves respect just as much as life already born.

In the Catholic tradition, this unborn life has been considered innocent life, and so its death can never be directly caused. The only situations in which taking the unborn life could be justified were those procedures in which the killing of the fetus was indirect and not intended. Chapter two presented the case of the cancerous uterus as an example of such a situation.

As we also saw in chapter two, however, this focus on the direct/indirect distinction cannot withstand careful analysis. What emerged as morally significant was the presence or absence of a sufficient reason. We might note that the advance of technology also undermined the usefulness of the direct/indirect distinction. Relying solely on indirect methods leads to absurd conclusions. Take, for example, the case of an ectopic pregnancy, in which the new life begins to develop in the fallopian tube rather than the uterus. Not only will the embryo not survive, it also threatens the mother's life.

The indirect method would require removing the fallopian tube, arguing that the death of the new life is indirect—what is intended is the removing of the "threatening" tube. This method would argue against shelling out the tube (once that technology became available) because that would be a direct killing of the new life. Clearly, in a case where the new life cannot survive and the mother's life is at stake, it only makes sense to choose the procedure that causes less harm to the mother. The discerning methodology presented in chapter two would, of course, argue in just this way.

The key determining factor, then, is presence or absence of a sufficient reason (again, not in one's desires, but in reality!). As we saw in the self-defense and just war examples in chapter two, the Christian tradition has recognized situations when life can be taken. Many people would likewise argue today that abortion can be justified only if human life is at stake. As we saw in those earlier examples, however, it is not always simply one life or another. In the case of a just war, the tradition allowed the taking of life to protect the freedom of a country. Thus, the tradition points in the direction of the sufficient reason being life itself or a good comparable to life itself.

The morality of abortion, then, focuses our attention on the evaluation of this new life and on reasons sufficient for ending it. Some people in the ongoing discussion about abortion see this new life as living but disposable tissue. Others recognize the new human life as having claims, but insist that these claims can be overridden by a wide range of concerns of the mother and family. Still others hold that this human life is a person in the process of becoming and so ought to be protected in all but a few rare cases. Clearly, the Catholic tradition (and many others) recognizes the unique worth and dignity of human life in all its stages.

This variety of evaluations of fetal life reveals the possible alternatives in the abortion debate, alternatives passionately held and expressed. As we can see, these alternatives generally place greater emphasis either on the mother or on the new life. Indeed, we probably only truly appreciate the complexity of the abortion debate when we realize the profound dilemma that exists between the woman's rights and those of the unborn child. It would seem that to respect fully the woman's dignity demands that she have the right and freedom to control her own life (and so be determined neither by male domination nor by biological structure). This would imply the right of abortion. On the other hand, protecting fully the rights of the weak and defenseless of our society is a desire reflected in efforts to end racism, to provide health care, to care for the aged; but to protect the unborn, abortion must be prohibited. A profound dilemma indeed!

A Response to the Dilemma

A response rooted in the first chapters of this book might approach the dilemma this way: Commitment to the Christian understanding of the truly human requires respect for all the beings involved: mother, father, fetus. Each is created in God's image. To be clear: This is true also for the new fetal life. Because life is sacred and fundamental, most goods (such as privacy, convenience, careers and so on) do not qualify as sufficient reason for ending the new life. Only life itself could be a sufficient reason.

What about the woman's rights? Certainly this view must be taken very seriously, for the woman's dignity must also be respected. But unrestricted right to abortion is not an acceptable option for three reasons. First, the mother has other options. If the pregnancy causes psychological or physical (but not life-threatening) problems, care for spirit and body is available. If a career or education is interrupted, resuming that career or education is possible. Only two options are available for the unborn child: either life or death. A woman's right to choose is not eliminated but is limited by the claims of the fetal life. It must be acknowledged that for many women sufficient care and support may not be readily available. But this lack argues for the need of greater support systems (from church and government agencies) rather than for the unrestricted right to abortion.

A second reason also underlines the mother's rights and responsibilities: her freedom to engage in sexual intercourse. Such a free choice implies certain responsibilities, including accepting the possibility of pregnancy. In the tragic case of rape, immediate medical treatment can prevent fertilization and ward off infection. In the rare event of a pregnancy resulting from rape, abortion still cannot be permitted, for life still has the greater claim. In such a situation, appropriate counseling and support for the woman would surely be essential.

The third reason for limiting abortion is similar to the argument in chapter two about the sheriff's dilemma of framing an innocent person to prevent a riot. Concerning abortion, a woman's dignity and right to control her life is finally contradicted by the unrestricted right to abortion. To undermine life through abortion is to undermine human freedom and dignity.

The suggested response, based on the first chapters of the book, also acknowledges the dignity of the father. In the United States at present, the father is practically powerless regarding the mother's choices about her pregnancy—including abortion. Yet morally he shares responsibility with her before, during and after the pregnancy. Before the pregnancy, the man must also act responsibly, considering the possible effects of sexual activity. If pregnancy occurs, he must participate in the decision-making. After birth he needs to support both mother and child in whatever ways he can.

The Legal Issue

Recognizing the profound dilemma between a woman's rights and those of an unborn child naturally leads us to the consideration of the legal aspects of the abortion debate. Again, it is helpful to recall the distinction between morality and legality: Even though an action is legal, it may not be moral. Morality focuses on our basic questions of "What ought I/we to do?" and "What ought I/we to be?"—that is, on the rightness or wrongness of human action. Law is concerned with the welfare of the community, the common good. Clearly the welfare of the community cannot be completely separated from what nurtures or destroys the individual. However, not all personal acts have the same kind of consequences for the common good, and so every moral law need not also be expressed as civil law.

Some people see permissive abortion laws as an injustice to the unborn—something that clearly relates to the welfare of the community. Others judge that restrictive laws are an injustice to the woman, and therefore the abortion decision ought to be left to the individual.

In its 1973 decision legalizing abortion, *Roe v. Wade*, the Supreme Court decided in favor of the woman's rights. The woman's right to privacy, the majority opinion stated, includes the abortion decision. Specifically, the woman has an absolute right to abortion during the first three months of pregnancy. For the second three-month period, states can establish certain regulations to protect the mother's well-being. During the final three months, states can regulate and even prohibit abortion except in cases where it might be necessary to preserve the life or health (this was interpreted very loosely) of the mother.

The decision was criticized by many scholars, some saying that the Supreme Court was doing the job of Congress by legislating, others objecting to the Court's giving priority to the woman's right to privacy over the unborn's right to life. Nevertheless, in the years following 1973, the Supreme Court continued to reaffirm its position.

In 1989, however, in *Webster v. Reproductive Health Services*, the Supreme Court ruled in favor of Missouri's law restricting abortions. Future decisions may allow even more restrictions; indeed, *Roe v. Wade* itself may be overturned, though this now seems unlikely. Overturning this decision, however, only removes a constitutional ban on state restrictions on abortion. It would then be up to the people of the individual states, through their legislatures, to determine whether and how abortion is to be limited.

Although such a process is the appropriate way to develop public policy in the United States, past experience and present signs indicate that it will likely be a very difficult process, marked more by slogans and rhetoric than by reasoned discourse. Perhaps some compromise, acceptable to many though certainly not to all, can be worked out. For example, scholars familiar with the abortion debate point out that many people would agree that abortion is legally acceptable if the alternative is tragedy, but not acceptable if the alternative is inconvenience. Accordingly, legislation might allow abortions in the cases of rape, incest and serious danger to the mother's physical health. (Statistics show that abortions for these reasons account for a tiny percentage of the more than one million abortions each year in the United States.)

As we saw earlier, some of these cases may not be morally justified. In our pluralistic society, however, where the divisions concerning abortion are so very deep, it may not be feasible to enact stricter legislation. And, in considering public policy, feasibility is a necessary criterion. Government must determine whether the policy will be obeyed, whether it is enforceable or whether enforcement will cause greater social harm.

A RENEWED DEBATE

The issue of abortion returned to the headlines and political debate in 1996 with the discussion of the procedure called partial-birth abortion. In this procedure, the baby is almost entirely delivered (feet first), but then a vacuum hose is inserted to suck out the baby's brains.

Both the horror of the procedure and its minimal difference from infanticide led to a firestorm of protest. Discerning fact from fiction in the midst of the rhetoric was not always easy. Some of the reasons given to allow the procedure included: It may be necessary to save the mother's life in certain circumstances; it may be necessary to preserve the woman's future fertility; the anesthesia given to the mother actually kills the unborn baby; it is rarely done. Expert medical testimony, on the other hand, rejected all these reasons.

Eventually Congress voted to ban the procedure, but President Clinton vetoed the bill. The House voted to override the veto; the Senate did not have the votes to override. Although votes may change as Congress realigns, the entire partial-birth abortion argument highlights the depth of division in the country and the lack of reasoned discourse.

Promoting Life

Throughout the many years of debate on abortion, the bishops of the United States (along with many others) have taken a strong stand against abortion. Given their conviction that abortion is a moral evil, "an unspeakable crime," the bishops have urged in their pastoral letters and in congressional testimony that the unborn child's right to life be recognized and fully protected by law. In urging constitutional protection of the right to life for the unborn, the bishops stress that they are not attempting to impose Catholic moral teaching on the country. Rather, they are defending human rights, just as in cases involving civil rights and antipoverty legislation. The bishops emphasize the responsibility of law and government to protect human rights, especially those of minorities who can be easily ignored.

Issues related to abortion have also drawn the bishops' attention. Simply to say no to abortion is not enough. Care must be given both to supporting women facing problem pregnancies and to the larger social evils such as sexism, poverty and racism, which may drive women to consider abortion as the only alternative. In dealing with these related issues, the bishops recognize the important role of local social service, health care and adoption agencies.

The commitment to life also extends to many other life issues: nuclear war, capital punishment, hunger, homelessness and health care. A systemic vision of promoting life pastorally contributes to the witness of the church's defense of the human being and publicly fills a void in the present policy debates in the United States. (We will consider several of these problems in more detail in the next two chapters.)

It is evident that abortion will continue to challenge us as a moral and public policy issue, a profound dilemma for individuals and for the nation. Our discerning methodology, rooted in the Christian tradition, provides a solid foundation both for moral clarity and commitment and for involvement in the dialogue about public policy concerning abortion.

Birth Control

In 1968 a papal encyclical addressed the topic of artificial contraception. Popes and bishops have frequently repeated the position of *Humanae Vitae*. Yet surveys continue to show that there exists widespread disagreement—even disregard—among Catholics concerning the teaching on birth control. Some scholars have noted that the birth control encyclical marked the first serious erosion of acceptance of official teaching, the beginning of the crisis of credibility. Some individuals, however, still struggle with feelings of guilt, while others feel caught trying to balance love, family size, money, church teaching and health. Artificial contraception clearly represents a complex and significant concern.

Papal Teachings and Public Reactions

What, then, can and must be said about contraception? Briefly recalling chapter three, we note that *Humanae Vitae*, although not infallible, provides authoritative guidance for the Catholic community (like other official teaching). Believing that the Spirit guides the pope and bishops as they carry out their role as official teachers, we presume the teaching is true. This does not mean, however, that the positions taken by the teaching do not need to be supported by good reasons. Nor does it excuse us from perfecting our own understanding or finding reasons that persuade us. But let's look at the official teaching.

In *Humanae Vitae*, Pope Paul VI reminded us of some very important values: human dignity, the meaning of sexuality, conjugal love and responsible parenthood. Unfortunately, the discussion of these values has been often overshadowed by the debate concerning artificial means of birth control. On this specific issue Paul held that a contraceptive act is intrinsically evil, that is, one that cannot be justified for any reason. The pope based this teaching on his understanding of sexual intercourse as a single act with two meanings, the unitive (mutual affection and the love-giving dimension of intercourse) and the procreative (the life-giving dimension).

According to the encyclical, these two meanings cannot be separated. Intercourse is to express love and be open to the transmission of life. Therefore, artificial contraception, in cutting off the procreative meaning, is evil because it involves a positive action against the possibility of life. Taking advantage of the body's natural rhythms of fertility and infertility, on the other hand, does not include such a positive act. Thus, the methods of natural family planning are morally acceptable because they remain attuned to both the unitive and procreative intent of sexual intercourse.

The prohibition against artificial means of birth control was reaffirmed by Pope John Paul II. Following the 1980 Synod of Bishops, which focused on the family, the pope published a lengthy exhortation (*Familiaris Consortio*) about marriage and family. In this wider context, he described contraception as a denial of the inner truth of conjugal love: It contradicts the total self-giving of husband and wife. On the other hand, he accepted natural family planning methods because this choice encouraged the values of dialogue, reciprocal respect, shared responsibility and self-control. For John Paul, these values represented a fundamentally different concept of the person and of human sexuality than that expressed by contraception.

The reactions to the papal teachings have been strikingly varied, ranging from "Rome has spoken; now all we have to do is obey" to "No educated Catholic will take this seriously." As frequently happens, such extreme reactions reveal more emotion than enlightenment. There were also careful responses to *Humanae Vitae*, however. These, too, varied in their reaction to Pope Paul VI's position.

Different national conferences of bishops explained *Humanae Vitae* in different ways, often showing deep respect for personal conscience. For example, the German bishops wrote: "Pastors must respect the responsible decisions of conscience made by the faithful." The Scandinavian bishops wrote:

No one, including the church, can absolve anyone from the obligation to follow his conscience....If someone for weighty and well-considered reasons cannot become convinced by the argumentation of the encyclical, it has always been conceded that he is allowed to have a different view from that presented in a non-infallible statement of the church. No one should be considered a bad Catholic because he is of such a dissenting opinion.

In *Human Life in Our Day*, the bishops of the United States described Paul's encyclical as "a defense of life and of love, a defense which challenges the prevailing spirit of the times" (27). The bishops go on: "It presents without ambiguity, doubt or hesitation the authentic teaching of the church concerning the objective evil of that contraception that closes the marital act to the transmission of life, deliberately making it unfruitful" (28).

A similar variety of responses was expressed by theologians from around the world. Many prominent moral theologians offered this kind of thoughtful and respectful response: The analysis in *Humanae Vitae* accepted biological structure and the processes of nature as the key for determining what is moral or immoral. Following Vatican II, however, they insisted that the basic criterion for the meaning of human actions is the total person and not just one aspect (the biological dimension) of the person.

In determining the morality of contraception, they said, the totality of the marriage—the relationships between husband and wife and with their children, the expression of the total dedication of love and the development of human dignity—must all be considered, and not just the biological process. In their judgment, *Humanae Vitae* did not sufficiently consider these developments in moral theology but simply repeated traditional understandings. Recent debates about contraception have continued along these same lines.

Contraception and the Search for Truth

So where does all this lead us? What does one make of official teachings, respectful questioning and the statistics about birth control that appear in the news? What about personal problems and tensions?

It leads, of course, to conscience and to that mature responsibility that searches for the truth of the moral dilemma. The issue of contraception provides an excellent example of the process described in chapter three, the dialogue between conscience and authority.

People who ponder the issue of birth control responsibly begin with an inner conviction that they should do good and avoid evil. Then they search for the right course of action and finally make a decision. But searching for the right thing to do has not been so clear or easy for some couples, especially for those who feel caught between opposing values. For example, they desire to respect the church's teaching. They desire to be open to conceiving new life. But they may also be concerned about their spouse's physical and emotional health, as well as for the educational, emotional and material needs of their children. Responsibility pulls in two different directions and yet a choice must be made. Contraception presents a very serious dilemma that cannot be casually resolved.

The challenge of mature decision-making demands simply that we do our best. Again, we recall that following our conscience does not mean simply doing what we want to do. No, it means searching for the truth, trying to discern God's will, even in situations of conflict, and being open to reaching a conclusion that we did not prefer.

So what is involved in this particular search? A couple must try to consult as widely as possible. This means carefully reading what Vatican II, *Humanae Vitae*, the popes and bishops have said about marriage and about contraception. Within the Catholic context, this official teaching demands special respect. The conviction of our faith is that official teaching also rests on the soundness of the reasons given, which therefore must be considered carefully. The guidance of the official teachers is ordinarily presumed to be true, but in particular cases there can be, and have been, changes in the church's understanding.

A conscientious search for the truth would naturally include an examination of how national conferences of bishops and respected theologians, thoughtful married couples and others have interpreted and struggled with *Humanae Vitae*. Of course, another part of the search is the consideration of the couple's own experience. Their own very real questions and tensions and hopes are important. They must try to be honest about all dimensions of their family life—both the positive (such as love and nurture of each other) and the negative (such as the selfish desire for more consumer goods and a more affluent lifestyle). This means they must honestly assess their own capabilities and limitations: How many children can they not only financially support but also realistically love and nurture? What is the state of the relationship with the spouse, and what best nourishes and supports this love? What are the physical and psychological states of all involved? This may not always be crystal clear.

Coming to a conclusion about the use of contraception is not just a matter of calculating advantages and disadvantages; the process does not fit into a mathematical equation. The search for truth in living the full meaning of Christian marriage also implies prayer, patience, humility and trust. In the search there must be an attitude of openness and attentiveness to God's call.

Making the Decision

No one can search and search and search endlessly—even though some of us desire to have everything perfectly clear and distinct! A decision must be made (the third dimension of conscience). We must make that decision. We must follow it. Although the pope, bishops and counselors can give valuable guidance, only the couple themselves can make the decision, which they come to after doing their very best in searching for truth.

A Catholic couple might face conflicting values, which seemingly cannot be attained simultaneously—for example, physical and psychological health, openness to new life, expressing and nurturing love for one's spouse, respecting the church's teaching. After weighing the alternatives and recognizing that apparently every value cannot be achieved at that particular moment in their marriage, the couple chooses the action which best expresses the meaning of Christian marriage.

If the couple decides that some form of family limitation is necessary, then a careful study of available means is important. Following not only the guidance of authority but also the positive experience of many couples, they will begin by learning what exactly natural family planning is. Recent advances have made this method very reliable for more and more couples, and many value its holistic approach. Unlike the older rhythm method, natural family planning is founded on sound scientific principles. It carefully monitors changes in temperature and other symptoms to determine fertile and infertile periods. (Many materials are available to explain this method in detail.)

Some couples may not find the natural method possible for physical or psychological reasons. These couples, as they try to embody the values of *Humanae Vitae* and as they struggle with their conflict situation, may sincerely decide that the most responsible choice for them is to explore artificial means of contraception. These couples must certainly be aware that some forms are abortifacient (that is, cause an abortion) rather than contraceptive (preventing conception). Clearly, we have two distinct issues here and much caution is required. Likewise recent studies have raised questions about side effects that some forms of birth control have on one's health. This, too, calls for careful attention.

Of course, this whole process of decision-making points to an issue much larger than what can be discussed here: communication between husband and wife. Obviously, the decision about family planning requires much dialogue. If spouses have different religious and moral views, this dialogue may well be more difficult. The potential (or real) conflict is one more element to be reflected upon as the couple try to reconcile different values and choose the best action.

Because of the depth of the dilemma and because of its close connections with ordinary life, contraception represents a profound challenge to mature moral reasoning and decision-making.

CATECHISM REFERENCES
Nos. 2258–2275, 2331–2379.

FOR REFLECTION AND DISCUSSION

1. Do you find evidence of prejudice concerning homosexuality in your neigh-borhood or city? What challenges does the gospel present our culture con-cerning the many forms of prejudice experienced by lesbian and gay per-sons? How has politics been involved with these issues?

2. Do you experience any prejudices toward gay and lesbian people? What is your reaction to the debated interpretations of Scripture? What will it take for you to risk the hard work of asking questions in a spirit of committed faithfulness?

3. Can abortion ever be justified? Why or why not? What realities must be included in the discussion about abortion? What are your reactions to this chapter's response to this profound moral dilemma?

4. How do you understand the distinction between legality and morality? Does this distinction enlighten the homosexuality and abortion debates? What do you consider to be the proper activity of politicians concerning public policy and same-sex marriages and abortion?

5. How would a systemic vision of promoting life influence public policy? How does it influence your life? Do individuals have the responsibility to change social structures and promote dialogue about public policy? How can you do that?

6. What civil or church agencies support pregnant women in your community? How can you be involved? Does your attitude toward out-of-wedlock pregnancies support or discourage a decision for abortion? What concrete steps can you take about the larger social issues (sexism, poverty, racism) which promote an abortion mentality?

7. Read Paul VI's *Humanae Vitae* (*On Human Life*). Reflect on some of the major themes of the encyclical: human dignity, the meaning of sexuality, responsible parenthood. How are these ideas related to your own life? What messages does our culture give us about these themes?

8. Recall chapter three's discussion about the proper response to non-infallible, authoritative teaching. How do you apply this to *Humanae Vitae*? What insights or questions do your reflections and experience bring to this issue?

chapter five

MEDICAL ETHICS

The rapid advance of medical technology has staggered our imaginations and challenged our moral sensitivities. What seemed to be science fiction only a short while ago is now reality. So many areas of medical research and care raise extremely complex dilemmas: test-tube conception, surrogate motherhood, artificial hearts, genetic engineering, euthanasia and health care itself. In this chapter we will concentrate on four of these issues that confront us as individuals and as a nation: stem-cell research, end-of-life issues (euthanasia, assisted suicide, the withdrawal of life-support systems), AIDS and the use of scarce resources and managed care.

STEM-CELL RESEARCH

The complex scientific and public policy issue of stem-cell research continues to raise serious and sensitive ethical questions. In this section we will briefly address three points: (1) What are stem cells? (2) What is the research? (3) What are the ethical dilemmas? Then we will consider several related issues, cloning and social justice.

1) Stem cells are basic building blocks of the human being. They possess the ability to develop in any number of directions: a heart, a liver, a brain, etc. Some stem cells (called "totipotent") have the ability to develop into a complete human organism. Other stem cells (called "pluripotent") can develop into multiple cell types. As we grow, however, the cells become specialized—some make up the heart, others the brain and so on.

2) Stem cells offer great potential for healing, including helping regenerate heart functions and treating diseases like Parkinson's and Alzheimer's. Not surprisingly, then, patient advocacy groups have joined many scientists in urging stem-cell research to learn more about this potential.

3) The ethical dilemmas center not on the research as such but on the source of the stem cells (and on the steps necessary to obtain the cells). Much of the research so far has focused on embryos. In the early stages of development, the cells of a human embryo are stem cells. Harvesting the cells means destroying the embryo. Other research makes use of stem cells found in umbilical cord blood and in bone marrow. (Some scientists have claimed that this latter research has, in fact, been much more successful.)

Clearly, then, the key ethical issue is the destruction of the embryo to obtain the stem cells.

What is an embryo? Simply "a collection of cells," as some researchers say? Or must we say more: The embryo is beginning human life with a unique genetic identity. It is not potential life; it is life with potential, needing only months of proper environment and nourishment to be born as a baby. Human life, then, deserves proper and appropriate respect (even if at the early stages the embryo may not yet be properly called a "person," because twinning is possible and we cannot split personhood into two—each twin is a unique person).

Destruction of beginning human life contradicts and undermines the value motivating the good cause of healing others, respect for life (see chapter two, page 25, on the meaning of sufficient reason). Calling the process "life affirming" does not make it so. In this situation, there are clearly other alternatives, even if choosing the ethical path (using the other sources of stem cells) may mean going at a slower or less efficient pace in research.

The fact that many of the embryos presently used in research are "leftovers" from fertility clinics does not change the morality of the act of destruction of the embryo. Rather, it raises the question of the morality of reproductive technology, especially fertilizing more eggs (for financial reasons, among others) than will be implanted.

Also, the use of "leftovers" points to a fundamental moral problem in the whole area: undermining our humanness. What is meant by "undermining our humanness"? Damaging or destroying dimensions of human life that through our experience, reflection and faith we have recognized as necessary for authentic life. Notice the language: People "make" and "use" embryos, they "experiment" on them and "discard" them.

Our advances in technology are truly wonderful but also problematic, especially with various forms of reproductive technology. The wonderful part is technology's capacity to help resolve and heal difficult and painful conditions. The problematic part is that the momentum of technological advance risks undermining our humanness. We make persons into things, human life into a commodity. Pulitzer Prize winner Jim Borgman expressed it perfectly in one of his editorial cartoons: The woman was ordering on the phone from "The Genome Barn" catalog. She said, "Yes, I'd like to order item number 94773-B, the do-it-yourself chromosome manipulation makeover kit with the cloning adaptor....Oh, and, what the heck, a set of frozen identical twins, in blonde." Beginning human life is no longer an awesome gift of God but a product of our hands.

Cloning

Besides using embryos from fertility clinics, researchers can also use cloning as a source. The process of "cloning" takes a cell from adult tissue and combines it with an unfertilized egg previously stripped of its genetic code, eventually developing a new being. Cloning can be used to produce new animals (the sheep named Dolly was a famous example) and perhaps humans some day. It can also produce embryos for stem-cell research; this process is usually called "therapeutic cloning."

Some researchers and activists claim the positive potential of cloning for the study and treatment of genetic diseases. Others feel that the process has horrendous implications, especially for human beings. Rhetoric about playing God and tampering with nature often surrounds the issue.

So, what can and ought Christian ethics say about cloning? First, two preliminary observations: (1) Ethical reflection must be based on clear understanding of what is happening—in this case, the process of cloning; (2) rhetoric may stir people's reactions, but often it is not enlightening. In this case, charges of tampering with nature convey the individual's response to cloning. But in fact we often change or adapt nature. Many of us wear glasses, for example. We have used technology to change nature, to help us see better.

Christian ethics, then, must look calmly and carefully at the issue of cloning, understand exactly what is going on, and weigh honestly both the benefits and the risks. Surely there are potential benefits, especially in studying and then treating certain kinds of diseases. There are serious risks as well, some of which are about cloning's impact (if it is applied to humans) on family and sexuality, on love and relationships. Christian ethics seeks to discover which action helps human life and all creation truly flourish.

In the case of cloning as with using "leftover" embryos, many people see that the greatest risk is actually undermining our humanness and that this risk far outweighs the benefits. From a Christian perspective, we believe human beings to be sacred, to be images of God—not manufactured goods or merely a product of technology. Life belongs to God; we are to respect it and care for it, but we do not have absolute control over it. Human cloning would cross this line.

SOCIAL JUSTICE

Both embryonic stem-cell research and cloning raise questions about the use of resources, profound social justice dilemmas often overlooked in this discussion. Our country (indeed, the world) does not have the time, talent, and treasure to do everything we need to do, much less everything we want to do. So priorities must be determined. Catholic teaching has long stressed the importance of the universal common good (see the last section of this chapter and also chapter six), so our vision must be very wide!

This social justice perspective includes various concerns about resources. With only a few companies holding many of the patents in stem-cell research, the potential for profit is enormous. Who will make the decisions and why? What role will "market forces" play? Another concern is who benefits from the results, in a country where millions do not have medical insurance and in a world where the gap between the "haves" and the "have nots" is increasing. Will cloning lead to new possibilities of attempting to create a master race or to increasing the inequalities among peoples?

Many people apparently have difficulty considering the moral implications of systemic issues, especially economic ones. However, the long social justice tradition that includes the prophets and Jesus (see page 131) calls us to face these challenges. Careful moral discernment in light of this tradition leads to the conclusion that we must consider investing more of our resources as a society in research related to urgent and more basic needs, such as basic health care and worldwide hunger.

This may sound harsh to those who are suffering from diseases possibly helped by stem-cell research or cloning. Surely it is not meant to be that; rather it is meant to recognize reality by stretching our vision to include the hundreds of millions of our sisters and brothers who not only face many diseases but also have little food and clean water.

This debate about stem cells and cloning, along with questions about humanness, public policy and the just sharing of resources, reminds us of the blessings and the threats of our technological age.

Issues at the End of Life

Euthanasia (mercy killing) and assisted suicide have become hotly debated issues in our society. Like abortion and stem-cell research, these issues confront us as both moral and legal dilemmas. The related but distinct question of withdrawing life-support systems is also part of this whole discussion. These end-of-life topics touch the depths of our being, stir the emotions and raise profound questions—and so call for careful moral reasoning.

In recent years, we have heard about alarming rates of murder/suicide among the elderly. Jack Kevorkian once frequently made headlines by helping people commit suicide. Physicians and ethicists have published careful guidelines for permitting euthanasia. Magazines and television shows have subtly supported "the right to die." Moral debates and legal battles have swirled around the question of withdrawing life-support systems. States have attempted to pass laws legalizing physician-assisted suicide and euthanasia; the Supreme Court has considered this very issue.

Responding to Euthanasia and Assisted Suicide

A nuanced response to these troubling and tragic events must begin by acknowledging the pain and mystery of suffering and dying. The fears that fuel the movement toward euthanasia must also be recognized and dealt with: fear of being a burden on one's family, fear of unbearable pain, fear of exhausting one's savings, fear of prolonging dying with tubes and machines.

The Bible provides a sound foundation and sure direction as we wrestle with these complex issues and fears. However, in turning to the Scriptures for guidance concerning such difficult and emotional decisions, we must remember that the Bible by itself will not be able to give all the answers. Quite simply, neither Moses nor Jesus had to worry about respirators and feeding tubes! But they did think about life, its meaning and its limits. Three major points emerge from the Scriptures: First, life is a basic (but not absolute) good; second, we are to be stewards of life, but we do not have complete control; third, we understand death in the context of belief in new life.

First, in Genesis, we hear of the goodness of all creation. The sacredness of human life is especially emphasized, for humans are created in God's image. Human life, then, possesses a dignity rooted in who we are rather than in what we do. Life is holy, deserving of respect and reverence. We know from our experience that life is the foundation for all other goods: friendship, love, prayer and all the other ways we enjoy and serve God and neighbor. Life, however, is not the most important good: Greater even than life is our relationship with God. We would not, for example, destroy our relationship with God through sin in order to save our physical life. The powerful witness of the martyrs testifies to this truth. Jesus himself embodied this truth in his teaching and living; he trusted in God and remained faithful even to death on a cross. Scripture makes it clear that life is a basic good but not an absolute one.

Second, stewardship must be distinguished from unlimited and absolute control. *Stewardship* implies that we have the responsibility to care for something that is not totally our own possession. *Control*, on the other hand, claims a radical and ultimate freedom or right to do whatever one wants. Beginning with Genesis, the Scriptures tell us again and again that we have stewardship over life, but never absolute control. Life belongs to God; it is to be respected and reverenced.

> To be stewards means to care for, to foster and nourish the gift of life—our own and that of others—so that our lives might flourish abundantly. Because we have been fashioned in the image of the Creator, we are, in a sense, "co-creators." (*Hopes and Fears: Pastoral Reflections on Death*, by the Ohio Catholic Conference of Bishops)

Jesus' whole life modeled the ideal of stewardship, creatively nourishing the gift of life and humbly accepting that pain and suffering cannot always be eliminated.

Third, the Scriptures offer us the conviction that death is not the final word. Death is not a transition from life to nothingness; rather, death marks the transformation to new and eternal life. This belief does not deny the reality of death, nor does it deny the suffering and separation that are part of that reality. This belief promises that life is changed, not ended. We can look forward in holy hope to the fullness of life.

Our belief in everlasting life is rooted, of course, in the transforming experience of the resurrection of Jesus. This resurrection faith allows us to see that new life comes through death. We, too, trust in God's loving faithfulness.

How, then, do these three biblical insights—life is a basic but not absolute good; we are stewards of life; death is not the final word—enlighten the dilemmas of euthanasia, assisted suicide and the use of life-support systems?

The conviction that we are stewards of life is basic to opposition to euthanasia. We use our creativity to cure illness and promote wellness. As stewards, we respond with care and compassion to those who are suffering. Indeed, we have much to learn about better methods of pain control; the example and work of the hospice movement has been particularly helpful in this area. As stewards, we also acknowledge that we face limits, that not all pain can be eliminated and ultimately death cannot be avoided. Mercy killing, however, moves beyond stewardship. Euthanasia, even for compassionate reasons, implies that we have absolute control over life and so contradicts who we are as "co-creators," who we "ought to be."

Similarly with assisted suicide, recognizing both the good gift of life and our responsibilities as stewards prohibits choosing suicide or helping someone else to end his or her life. Suicide, though rooted in frustration, pain and despair, is an attempt to seize ultimate control over life. It contradicts the fundamental reality of our lives.

Citizenship and Public Policy

The decision for euthanasia or assisted suicide may seem to be very private, yet it has profound implications for society. Certainly the movement to legalize euthanasia and assisted suicide has brought the issues into the public forum. Public opinion polls often indicate widespread support, which may be based more on an emotional response than on careful reasoning.

While the discussions about legalizing continue, it will be necessary for those opposed to euthanasia on religious grounds to work with others who are also opposed but for other reasons. Many are convinced that legalizing euthanasia and assisted suicide would further undermine reverence for life in our society, would reduce trust in the medical profession and would put old and infirm people in vulnerable positions. A number of feminists have pointed out that women would especially be at risk, given society's history of oppression of women and given that women live longer than men but have fewer financial and social resources.

As in the abortion debate, the public policy dimensions of the euthanasia issue are serious and demand an intelligent, nuanced response that respects the dignity of all persons. In their moral reflection, *Faithful for Life*, the United States bishops emphasize Christian fidelity and then civic responsibility:

> But we are also citizens, and we share the right—indeed, the duty—of all citizens to insist that the laws and policies of the United States be faithful to our founders' conviction that the foremost "inalienable right" conferred by our Creator on all of us is life itself. When disadvantaged or disenfranchised people have their pursuit of happiness, their liberty, and even their lives threatened by their nearest neighbors, we are bound to stand up for them and with them.

Withdrawing Life-Support Systems

The question of withdrawing or withholding life-support systems is distinct from (and yet often associated with) the question of euthanasia. Making decisions concerning another person's dying can be especially difficult. Yet many people have had to decide whether or not to withdraw life-support systems from a loved one who was dying. As our technology improves, the number of these situations will increase even more. Withdrawing life-support systems—such things as respirators and feeding tubes—is a wrenching decision.

There was a tragic case in Chicago: A distraught father entered the hospital with a gun, kept people away as he turned off the machines that were keeping his comatose toddler alive and held the child until he died. Surely we cannot condone the use of such force. Just as surely, we realize that the situation should never have reached such a stage.

Fortunately, reflection and experience have helped us to discern when such things as respirators do not need to be used. Unfortunately, legal issues continue to complicate such situations as the one in Chicago. The moral obligation to preserve or prolong life ceases if prolonging life really does not help the person in striving for the purpose of life. Later we will return to this topic in greater detail; for now, perhaps an example will help.

If someone has a heart attack, that person may well need the assistance of a respirator to carry the person through the crisis period. At that point there is reasonable hope of recovery and return to more-or-less normal life. In such a situation, life ought to be prolonged; the respirator ought to be used.

On the other hand, if a person is in a permanent coma or a persistent vegetative state with no real hope of any kind of recovery, then the obligation to prolong life through mechanical means such as a respirator ceases. Note that at the beginning the person would be put on a respirator when there is hope of recovery. Once it is determined that there is no reasonable hope of recovery, the respirator can be removed.

More serious questions, however, surround the use of providing nourishment and fluids by medical means. Our consideration of this dilemma also gives us the opportunity to expand the earlier brief statement on prolonging life. Two cases that received national attention will help us focus on the important issues concerning withdrawing these life-support systems.

Paul Brophy was a forty-six-year-old Massachusetts firefighter when he underwent emergency brain surgery. He never recovered consciousness after the operation and entered a vegetative state, unable voluntarily to control his muscles or to respond to verbal statements. Medical experts considered Brophy's condition irreversible. Apart from severe brain damage, Brophy's health was good. He was not in danger of imminent death, and perhaps could have lived for years with continued feeding through a tube inserted into his stomach. On several occasions before the surgery, he had expressed his conviction that he did not want to be put on a life-support system. After Brophy persisted in this vegetative state for over a year, Patricia Brophy, his wife, requested that the tube feeding end because he had no quality of life remaining.

Claire Conroy was an eighty-four-year-old resident in a nursing home. She suffered from irreversible mental and physical problems, including heart disease, diabetes and hypertension. She was unable to swallow and was fed by a tube through her nose. Though she would smile or moan in response to some stimuli, she could not speak. Her movements were very limited; she was restricted to a semi-fetal position. Thomas Whittemore, Miss Conroy's nephew and guardian, requested that the feeding tube be removed from his awake but severely mentally incapacitated aunt.

The Moral Dilemma

Ethical reflection on these cases centers on the removal of the feeding tubes. The basic question that emerges is this: Is withholding or withdrawing artificial hydration and nutrition killing the person or simply allowing the person to die (that is, not needlessly interfering with the dying process)? Related to this fundamental question are several others. Is artificial hydration and nutrition a medical procedure? When nutrition and hydration are withdrawn, are we intending death for the patient?

One other point should be noted about the Brophy and Conroy cases. Not surprisingly, both cases were taken to the courts. In both cases decisions were made and overturned. Civil law will continue to be an important aspect of this whole discussion. As we saw in the discussion about abortion, many moral issues are significant enough to warrant passing civil laws to promote the common good. Many bioethical issues fall into this category. Law also complicates matters. In this section, however, we will concentrate on the moral questions.

To do careful moral analysis, we must consider some of the language and concepts used in the discussion about life support. Language is very important—yet, because it is also so familiar, we may miss built-in meanings, evaluations, even prejudices. Recall the distinction made in chapter two between killing and murder. Killing indicates that one person has ended the life of another. That is an unfortunate event, indeed an evil. But we do not know if it is a justified killing—self-defense, for example. If it is not justified, then we call that act "murder." The word *murder* describes the same physical act (one person ending the life of another), but also includes a moral evaluation: This was an unjustified act and therefore a moral evil.

Now look again at our basic question: Is the withdrawal of artificial hydration and nutrition killing the person or simply allowing the person to die? What is contained in this language? "Allowing to die" can be either justified or unjustified. Justified allowing to die means one does not needlessly interfere with the dying process; this implies a certain passivity, yet may include withdrawing life-support systems. Unjustified allowing to die means one fails to take steps that ought to be done, such as using the respirator in the heart attack case. This unjustified allowing to die is called killing—or more accurately, murder. Thus, the ethical dilemma we are analyzing can be expressed this way: When is the withdrawal of artificial nutrition and hydration justified and when is it not?

What about "nutrition and hydration"? Would "food and water" give a very different sense to our question? Does one phrase suggest a medical procedure and the other a basic human need; one some kind of medical device, the other a bowl of soup? Does our choice of words subtly determine our position and color our ethical reasoning?

Here consider two other extremely important concepts frequently used in evaluating life support: extraordinary and ordinary means. Probably a combination of effective communication and especially of common sense has led to the widespread appreciation of this distinction. One must make use of ordinary means of medical help; extraordinary means are optional. All kinds of folks—from the simple to the highly educated—find this distinction helpful in making moral decisions about medical issues.

There are, however, two problems. First, ethicists are not referring to medical procedures alone when they speak of "ordinary" and "extraordinary." They are speaking of the overall effort made to keep a person alive in relation to how those efforts will help the patient pursue life's purposes. Second, even if one equates the terms *ordinary* and *extraordinary* solely with medical procedures, as many people do, whether a procedure is ordinary or extraordinary depends upon what medical help is available in a given place. That distinction is continually changing as improved technology becomes available. What was extraordinary ten years ago is now quite ordinary. What is ordinary here in the United States is extraordinary in a Third World country.

Why do people continue to rely upon such ambiguous terms? Perhaps the words *ordinary* and *extraordinary* are used not so much to help reach a conclusion as to express a conclusion already decided. Like the word *murder*, these words carry along a built-in evaluation: *Ordinary* implies a judgment that these medical procedures ought to be done; *extraordinary* points to optional use.

Responses to the Dilemma

If we return to our fundamental question and ask whether artificial hydration and nutrition are ordinary or extraordinary means, the answer must be both. It depends on the total situation. If the distinction between extraordinary and ordinary means is not especially helpful, how then do we answer our basic question: When is the withdrawal of artificial nutrition and hydration justified? Let's look at three possible positions that are promoted in contemporary society.

1) *"Euthanasia is OK."* At one extreme we have those who support euthanasia. They endorse not only the withdrawal of artificial life support but even the active shortening of a patient's life, for example, by lethal injection.

Their position is based on strong emphasis on individual rights, with the concepts of "right to privacy," "self-determination" and "death with dignity" at the heart of their argument. This position is rejected by many, including the official teachings of the Catholic church.

2) *"Life must be sustained at all costs."* At the other extreme we have those who hold that the withdrawal of artificially provided food and fluids for people with even severe disabilities cannot be ethically justified except in very rare situations. The fundamental idea for this second position is the following: Remaining alive is never rightly regarded as a burden because human bodily life is inherently good, not merely instrumental to other goods. Therefore, it is never morally right deliberately to kill innocent human beings even by acts of omission such as the failure to provide adequate food and fluids. This second position emphasizes that the deliberate killing of the innocent, even if motivated by an anguished or merciful wish to end painful and burdened life, is not morally justified by that motive.

This position acknowledges that means of preserving life may be withheld or withdrawn if the treatment employed is judged either useless or excessively burdensome. Traditionally, a treatment has been judged useless if it offers no reasonable hope of benefit. A treatment has been judged excessively burdensome when whatever benefits it offers are not worth pursuing for some reason, such as it is too painful, too restrictive of the patient's liberty or too expensive.

Here is the significant point of this position: Given its presuppositions, this position holds that the "useless or excessive burden" criteria can be applied to the person who is imminently dying but not to those who are permanently unconscious (Paul Brophy) or to those who require medical nourishment as a result of something like Lou Gehrig's disease or Alzheimer's disease (Claire Conroy). Feeding these patients and providing them with fluids by means of tubes is not useless because it does bring these patients a great benefit: namely, the preservation of their lives.

Finally, this position recognizes that such care can be costly in time and energy. But such care provides benefits to the patient (life itself) and to the caregiver (an experience of mercy, compassion and appreciation of human dignity).

3) *"Life is a fundamental but not absolute good."* This approach attempts to find a middle path between these two extremes. On the one hand, it rejects

euthanasia, judging deliberate killing a violation of human dignity. On the other hand, while it values life as a great and fundamental good, life is not seen as an absolute (as we saw in the section of this chapter on scriptural foundations) to be sustained in every situation. Accordingly, in some situations, artificial nutrition and hydration may be removed.

This position, supported by the American Medical Association, states that the focus on imminent death may be misplaced. Instead we should ask if a disease or condition that will lead to death (a fatal pathology) is present. For example, a patient in an irreversible coma cannot eat and swallow and thus will die of that pathology in a short time unless life-prolonging devices are used. Withholding artificial hydration and nutrition from a patient in an irreversible coma does not cause a new fatal disease or condition. It simply allows an already existing fatal pathology to take its natural course. Here, then, is a fundamental idea of this third position: If a fatal condition is present, the ethical question we must ask is whether there is a moral obligation to seek to remove or bypass the fatal pathology.

But how do we decide either to treat a fatal pathology or to let it take its natural course? Life is a great and fundamental good, a necessary condition for pursuing life's purposes: happiness, fulfillment, love of God and neighbor. But does the obligation to prolong life ever cease? Yes, if prolonging life does not help the person strive for the purposes of life. Pursuing life's purposes implies some ability to function at the level of reasoning, relating and communicating. If efforts to restore this cognitive-affective function can be judged useless or would result in profound frustration (that is, a severe burden) in pursuing the purposes of life, then the ethical obligation to prolong life is no longer present. It is important to note that the "severe burden" refers to pursuing the purposes of life, not the means to prolong life.

This third approach recognizes that making decisions for others is especially difficult. In such situations we must realize that many persons with limited bodily and spiritual function can still pursue the purposes of life. Thus, simply because a person is seriously impaired does not automatically imply that this person can be allowed to die from an existing fatal pathology. Finally, even the person who has physiological function but no hope of recovering cognitive-affective function is still a human being and so deserves comfort care.

Disagreements in the Church

How are these three significantly different positions judged by the Roman Catholic church? The Catholic position (as we have already seen) has consistently opposed euthanasia. But there is no definitive Catholic position regarding the other two approaches to our topic. Vatican commissions and Catholic bishops' conferences have come down on both sides of the issue. Likewise, there are Catholic moral theologians on both sides.

In an attempt to respond to this controversy, the Committee for Pro-Life Activities of the National Conference of Catholic Bishops issued *Nutrition and Hydration: Moral and Pastoral Reflections* in 1992. This statement called for a presumption in favor of using medically assisted nutrition and hydration, but added that it may be removed in certain circumstances, e.g., when burdens outweigh benefits. This guidance was then included in the bishops' *Ethical and Religious Directives for Catholic Health Care Services.*

In 2004 Pope John Paul II, speaking at a Vatican conference, seemed to disagree with the U.S. bishops' statements by opposing the removal of medically assisted nutrition and hydration ("seemed" because there is debate about whether the pope allowed removal in some circumstances). Moreover, proper respect for papal pronouncements, as explained in chapter three, understands that this kind of statement must be taken seriously, but it is neither infallible nor the final word.

Profound disagreement about end-of-life ethics still exists in the church. In 2005 another famous end-of-life case, the removal of the feeding tube from Terri Schiavo, a woman in a persistent vegetative state, highlighted the confusion. Legality and morality were very publicly debated. Responses moved more toward polarization than toward an informed consideration of the medical facts and a careful search for the moral truth. Such a search, however, remains a moral imperative of utmost urgency.

Conclusion with Cautions

The discerning methodology presented in the first three chapters corresponds very closely to the third position. Let's return to our basic question: Is the withdrawal of artificial nutrition and hydration killing a person or simply allowing the person to die? The discerning answer must be: It depends. If a fatal pathology is present and if life-prolonging efforts would be useless or a severe burden in pursuing the purpose of life, then the answer to our question is "allowing to die." In this kind of situation we are not intending death by starving the person, but merely allowing the pathology to take its normal course. This conclusion can be expressed in other words: When a fatal disease or condition is present and when life-prolonging efforts would be useless in pursuing the purposes of life, then there is a sufficient reason for withdrawing medical nourishment.

In the cases of Paul Brophy, Claire Conroy and Terri Schiavo, for example, the discerning method would likely reach just this conclusion. The reality of life is recognized as a fundamental but not absolute good. Human dignity is fully respected and appreciated. Death is not the ultimate evil; alienation from God is. Though not without sorrow, death marks the passage to new life. God is the source and goal of our life.

Two important cautions must be mentioned. First, euthanasia has always provided a challenge for careful moral reasoning. In many cases euthanasia does seem to be the merciful response. Would it not be more merciful to hasten the death of someone in great pain? There is an emotional tug here. However strong that tug, the discerning methodology finds a profound difference between allowing to die and causing death—a difference not for the patient but for us, the doers of the action. Taking life in this situation, even though for a good motive, is an action that will undermine our humanity. It is a line we ought not to cross.

Second, our society too easily evaluates people in terms of their productivity. We must be careful to proclaim the unique value of each person and to protect the rights of people with physical handicaps, mental illnesses and disabilities or other special needs.

HIV/AIDS

"The crisis continues, but it can be met with understanding, justice, reason, and deep faith." In the years since the U.S. bishops concluded their 1989 *Called to Compassion and Responsibility* on the AIDS epidemic with these words, there have been many life-giving expressions of understanding and reason, many hopeful signs of deep faith. During this time, however, the crisis not only continued but grew much worse.

Now a growing numbness about HIV and AIDS infects many people in resource-rich countries. We fail to recognize that the AIDS epidemic is spreading ominously in the world's most populous countries, India and China. HIV/AIDS remains a global issue of immense importance, requiring careful reflection, faithful prayer and committed action.

Our numbness may actually begin in success, the success of the antiretroviral drug therapy that improves significantly the lives of those infected with HIV. As a result, AIDS disappears from the headlines and from our consciousness. Other sources of our numbness may be a weariness with the harsh reality of AIDS in the developing countries or, on the other hand, a lack of awareness of these situations. Perhaps even some prejudice or judgment that AIDS is an expression of God's wrath causes us to turn away.

AIDS and Suffering

Let's first recall some basic facts about this deadly infection. AIDS (Acquired Immune Deficiency Syndrome) is caused by HIV (Human Immunodeficiency Virus). This virus attacks certain white blood cells called T cells, eventually destroying the person's immune system. As a result, the individual can suffer from many diseases that a healthy immune system would reject. One of these "opportunistic" infections finally kills the person.

The AIDS virus is spread in several ways: sexual contact (including heterosexual and homosexual intercourse), exchange of blood (especially by sharing dirty needles for drugs, tattoos or steroids; "dirty" means that the needle has already been used and contains some blood of an HIV-infected person), and the birth process (an infected mother can transmit the virus to her infant). HIV, then, is spread when certain body fluids are transferred from an infected person: in semen, vaginal fluids, blood, breast milk, as well as in the process of birth. HIV is not spread through casual contact. We must note that in one sense HIV is relatively hard to spread (only several means are possible), and yet these very means are found in ordinary activity (sexual intercourse) and in frequent addictive behavior (intravenous drug use).

Once infected with HIV, a person (called HIV-positive) is able to infect other persons, even though the infected person shows no signs of the disease. This latency period, the time from HIV infection to the development of AIDS, can last more than ten years. Just about everyone who is infected with HIV will develop AIDS, unless treated by antiretroviral drugs, the most effective being a combination called highly active antiretroviral therapy (HAART). For many persons these drugs stop the virus from replicating, transforming the infection into a chronic disease. This combination of drugs, however, does not completely eliminate the virus, so for the present, ongoing treatment remains necessary.

Some people experience very serious side effects from HAART. Another limitation, due to cost and corporate policies, is the harsh reality that this treatment is not available for the great percentage of the world's people infected with HIV. Also, work on an AIDS vaccine continues, but has not been successful because of the different strains of HIV and because the virus mutates so easily.

The spread of HIV and AIDS is staggering. Statistics constantly change, but the following numbers give some sense of the magnitude of this global epidemic. By 2005 an estimated 40 million people were living with HIV/AIDS. More than 20 million persons had already died, including 2.6 million just in 2003. Worldwide, the main cause of infection has been heterosexual intercourse. This fact led Pope John Paul II, in 1990, to comment to the bishops of Burundi that "the threat of AIDS now confronts our generations with the end of earthly life in a manner which is all the more overwhelming because it is linked, directly or indirectly, to the transmission of life and love." In some countries the epidemic begins with injecting drug use and then spreads through sexual contact.

HIV/AIDS is devastating the developing countries. Over 90 percent of persons with HIV live in these countries. Because of AIDS, nations already reeling from poverty, famine, war, and other diseases face many more deaths, reduction in the number of workers, greater economic and political instability. In the United States, HIV/AIDS is especially attacking the African-American and Hispanic communities.

Such sobering statistics have led AIDS researchers to conclude that wherever HIV enters a population, it always moves to those peoples who are already experiencing poverty, oppression, disease and marginalization. In the haunting words of Paul Farmer, M.D., HIV/AIDS has a "preferential option for the poor."

Misinformation

Addressing this overwhelming suffering is made much more difficult by the presence of widely accepted misconceptions. In wealthy countries both policy makers and ordinary citizens hold such theories as these: HIV/AIDS continues to spread in poor countries because people refuse to change their lifestyles. Antiretroviral treatments are too costly or technically impossible for developing countries. The only option is to concentrate on prevention, not treatment. An AIDS vaccine will soon be available. Ordinary people cannot confront the power of the big pharmaceutical companies. Wealthy countries have nothing to gain by fighting HIV and AIDS in the developing world.

Because many of us can get trapped by these false assumptions, we must be careful not to jump to conclusions too quickly. Serious analysis of such theories reveals how far from the truth they are. These false claims lead to passivity, pessimism and numbness. Accurate information, on the other hand, opens up the possibility of hope and committed action.

One example is the misconception that wealthy countries have nothing to gain. (This and other examples are discussed in *Global AIDS: Myths and Facts* by Alexander Irwin, Joyce Millen and Dorothy Fallows.) In countries like the U.S., working against the spread of HIV and AIDS can be motivated by national self-interest, especially in the areas of public health, economic growth and security. Globalization increases the possibility of more infections, so fighting HIV and AIDS elsewhere protects the future health of U.S. citizens. Helping insure productivity and profits in other countries now threatened by the impact of AIDS will produce economic returns in the U.S. AIDS also has political impact, creating destabilization and violence that spills over into the international community, threatening national security.

SIGNS OF DEEP FAITH

If we move beyond self-interest, we see that the strongest argument for dealing with AIDS is based on morality and spirituality. Since the beginning of the epidemic, the Catholic church has been actively involved in word and in deed. Based on the Bible and on the church's long tradition, the church's teachings have stressed (1) the value and dignity of every person, (2) the rights and responsibilities of society, (3) the love and compassion of God.

Many national conferences of bishops have issued statements concerning HIV/AIDS. In the United States, the Administrative Board of the U.S. Catholic Conference published *The Many Faces of AIDS: A Gospel Response* in 1987. The whole National Conference of Catholic Bishops published *Called to Compassion and Responsibility: A Response to the HIV/AIDS Crisis* in 1989. Since then individual bishops or groups of bishops have addressed their people. Similarly, Pope John Paul II regularly spoke about HIV/AIDS, either at AIDS conferences or during his visits to nations, especially those suffering from AIDS in a critical way.

The church has also directly responded to those suffering from HIV and AIDS. In fact, Catholic church-related organizations offer more AIDS care than any other institution in the world. This gift of faith is often overshadowed in the popular media by the debate concerning the morality of using condoms. This focus actually leads many people to develop a negative impression about the church's response to the crisis.

Many other expressions of deep faith, of course, are found in other individuals, institutions and religions.

Ethical Dilemmas

Staggering suffering and subtly seductive misconceptions present us with many ethical questions. They extend throughout the life span and cover the globe. Let's consider five clusters of moral issues in order to appreciate the complexity of ethical dilemmas raised by HIV/AIDS.

The first cluster is focused on birth and infancy. Ought HIV-infected women to become pregnant? Is contraception possible when AIDS is involved? What is the proper treatment for HIV-infected infants? How can society care for AIDS orphans?

A second cluster of ethical questions relates to HIV-infected persons and their relationships. What are their moral responsibilities concerning risky behavior which could infect others? Must previous contacts be informed? What about dealings with physicians: issues of privacy, confidentiality, truth-telling, using experimental drugs?

A third cluster centers on the end of life. How much pain must be endured? What kinds of life-support treatment are appropriate? Is there a limit to the resources to be used?

Society itself faces a fourth cluster of moral dilemmas. Does the common good of society demand testing for the AIDS virus, and who will be tested? How does society fund and manage research and testing? Is there a moral obligation concerning educational programs in the light of the growing epidemic? Should programs that promote the use of condoms or needle exchange be supported? What about the effects of prejudice against HIV-infected persons: in housing, parishes, employment, insurance and medical treatment?

The fifth cluster is perhaps the most challenging, the global structural issues. What ought societies do about the economic and social and political structures that contribute to the spread of AIDS? Poverty, racism, oppression of women, global economy, maximization of profits, forced migration, war and violence of all kinds create the perfect breeding grounds (risky sexual situations and the use of drugs) for the flourishing of the HIV/AIDS epidemic. What ought governments do, and how can individual persons help?

As stated earlier, the great percentage of the earth's HIV-positive people do not have access to the life-saving antiretroviral drugs. The roots of this situation lie in political and economic choices and structures. Some countries have chosen to violate international patent laws or to work out some kind of compromise in order to produce generic forms of the drugs at a much lower cost. Other countries are too poor even to do that.

For many people, especially those in developing countries, addressing these questions remains a great challenge, due to the lack of physical and personal resources. Freedom, for example, is often limited by cultural and economic conditions. Many women may be forced into sex with unfaithful and infected husbands or into prostitution to support their families. Ultimately then, confronting AIDS adequately demands addressing this fifth cluster of global structural issues.

LIGHT FOR OUR PATH

The harsh and horrible reality of global AIDS and this long list of disturbing ethical questions cry out for individual and systemic responses. And so we turn to our Scriptures and tradition for the foundation of our vision and for guidance for our action.

The Scriptures: Our ancient Bible guides our response to the modern AIDS epidemic: (1) by reminding us that AIDS is not a punishment sent by God; (2) by giving Jesus as an example of care and compassion; (3) by challenging us to question and change structures of society that oppress people.

1) Deeply embedded in some streams of Hebrew thought was the sense that good deeds led to blessing and evil deeds to suffering. If a person were experiencing sickness or other trials, then that person must have sinned in the past. The book of Job, however, challenges this tradition; Job suffers despite his innocence (Job 31 especially).

Jesus too challenges this belief. In the exquisite scene described in John 9, Jesus heals a blind man. Jesus declares that the man's blindness was not due to his or his parents' sin (John 9:2–5). Neither Job nor Jesus explains away the pain of suffering, but neither views sickness as a punishment from God.

2) Mark's Gospel (1:40–2) describes Jesus healing a leper (see also Matthew 8:1–4 and Luke 5:12–16). This event reveals not only Jesus' care for an individual in need but also his concern about structures of society. Jesus steps across the boundaries separating the unclean and actually touches the leper. In doing so, Jesus enters into the leper's isolation and becomes unclean. Human care and compassion, not cultural values of honor and shame, direct Jesus' action. He calls into question the purity code that alienates and oppresses people already in need.

3) Jesus' compassionate act of healing already points to societal issues. In this act, Jesus stands firmly in the prophetic tradition of the Bible. Again and again, the prophets challenged the people not to separate justice concerns from true religion. Isaiah powerfully expressed this conviction: "Is not this the fast that I choose: to loose the bonds of injustice, to undo the thongs of the yoke…? Is it not to share your bread with the hungry…?" (see Isaiah 58:1–12).

Jesus embodied and expressed this vision in his parables about God's reign and in his healings and table fellowship. His encounter with the leper is just one example of many.

The Tradition: The Catholic tradition, especially as articulated in recent social teachings (see chapter six), helps us to embody this biblical vision in our personal and political lives. Key themes from this tradition include human dignity, solidarity, justice and the common good.

Human dignity is the foundation of all the social teachings. Because all human beings are created in God's image, we are sacred and precious. Accordingly, all persons have worth and dignity, rooted simply in who they are (and not in what they do or achieve). All forms of discrimination are wrong, whether in housing, jobs, insurance, health care or religion.

Technology and globalization constantly remind us of the deeper interdependence of the human family. Many of Pope John Paul's writings emphasized this solidarity, especially with the poor of the world. He affirmed that the church follows God in expressing a preferential option for the poor. This option recognizes the power of economic and social structures to perpetuate poverty and limit personal freedom. The pope named such conditions "structures of sin."

Justice—right relationships along with the structural recognition of human dignity and rights and responsibilities—is another major theme emphasized throughout the social teachings. The Synod of Bishops in 1971 even called justice "a constitutive dimension of the preaching of the gospel."

The goal of justice is to create a global society where the common good flourishes. The common good, according to Blessed Pope John XXIII, means all those things necessary for all peoples to live truly human lives. What most of us take for granted—food, clothing, shelter, participation in religion and politics—is lacking in the lives of hundreds of millions of the human family.

OUR RESPONSE TO HIV/AIDS

Today many people infected with HIV and AIDS experience suffering, stigmatization and rejection. Societal powers make the situation worse. Throughout the world, economic systems and decisions trap people in poverty. Racism fosters oppression. Religion too often promotes judgmental attitudes. Violence and widespread denial of any real freedom force many people, especially women, into tragic situations.

How are we to respond? Clearly, our Scriptures and tradition challenge us to live as faithful disciples of Jesus. Our reflections have led us to three specific points concerning HIV and AIDS.

1) We resist the temptation to judge and condemn people. Stigmatization still happens. "In society, people treat us like lepers," states a person living with AIDS, "particularly people from the church. We listen to the beliefs and preaching, and so we hope to find acceptance, care and love. And that's just what we need—a community to belong to, a spirituality to help us keep going. But instead we are rejected." HIV/AIDS is not a punishment sent by God. This change of attitude is where we start. This respect does not mean, of course, denying responsibility. Prevention is still the key to dealing with HIV and AIDS, so creative and culturally-sensitive educational programs must encourage people to take responsibility for their actions.

2) We respond with care and compassion to those infected and affected by HIV, crossing the boundaries of fear and prejudice. With the attitude of Jesus, we reach out to these sisters and brothers. This means action, perhaps starting a parish support group or helping a local agency that assists those living with AIDS—or at least supporting those who do this.

3) We recognize the need for societal change as well as behavioral change. Recent social teachings of the church help us translate the vision of the prophets and Jesus into just working and living conditions. This too means action—systemic action. The consistent ethic of life guides us in accepting personal responsibility to challenge and change political platforms, economic strategies and governmental decisions that foster a culture of death.

Getting information, from the National Catholic AIDS Network or UNAIDS, for example, is a first step. Attention to politics is vital, by informed voting and pressuring leaders to support fully the Global Fund to Fight AIDS, Tuberculosis, and Malaria. For some people, actual participation in political and economic decisions is possible. Joining or supporting advocacy groups that promote local and global justice expresses one's solidarity with the poor. Economic issues deserve special work: challenging the policies and practices that limit access to HIV drug therapy, promoting debt relief for poor countries and resisting free-trade agreements (that do not treat the poor justly but do increase profits for the wealthy).

A response rooted in the social teachings recognizes the necessity of personal responsibility and also emphasizes the pervasive influence of these political, economic and social structures that contribute to the spread of HIV and AIDS. Only if the developed world addresses the global structural issues will conditions be changed so that personal freedom can truly be exercised and life can flourish throughout the world. This political and economic task may well be the most challenging, for the emphasis on justice and the common good calls into question some of the basic values and practices of the United States, especially economic ones.

Even as our numbness may be deepening, the deaths and suffering from AIDS continue, particularly in the developing countries. HIV/AIDS may rarely make the headlines these days, but it is devastating the lives of individuals and families, communities and countries. In the midst of this crisis, we are called to live and act as informed citizens and faithful disciples, with a spirituality of compassion and a passion for justice.

Scarce Resources and Managed Care

All of the topics considered in this chapter, stem-cell research, end-of-life issues and AIDS, point to an even greater health-care challenge: the allocation of scarce resources. This issue is foundational to all other medical dilemmas. For example, in some of the issues we just considered, a significant percentage of money and talent is invested in aggressive crisis intervention. Could this money and talent be better spent on basic and preventive care? Will there ever be enough resources to meet the needs of everyone? As the AIDS crisis worsens, who will treat the increasing numbers of indigent patients? What about other needs? And who pays the bill?

Public Expectations

The dramatic implications of this issue of resources are symbolized by the title of an article by James Childress: "Who Shall Live When Not All Can Live?" Yet within the United States, there exists a deeply held optimism about health care, which denies such a sober question. Medical technology has advanced tremendously; we are more and more confident that medicine can conquer disease and postpone death. We have seen it happen so often! Where solutions are yet to be found, we feel that we have the financial and human resources to devote to new discoveries. Where failures are acknowledged, we are convinced that efficiency and a greater use of technology will provide the necessary responses.

Scientific studies of public opinion (one by Louis Harris and Associates for the Loran Commission, another by the Public Agenda Foundation) demonstrate this confidence about health care along with a real concern for other people. These studies also reveal a glaring inconsistency. The great majority of Americans hold that every person has the right to get the best possible health care, that this best care can be constantly improved through research, that more can be spent on health care and yet at the same time the system can be more efficient, that the government ought to bear the costs of individuals' catastrophic illness. The great majority of people, however, rejected the possibility of a tax increase to pay for such catastrophic coverage. Our desires and expectations far exceed what we are willing to pay for. (See "Allocating Health Resources" by Daniel Callahan.)

Facts, however, contradict this optimism and direct our attention back to the urgent but harsh questions. Facts indicate that attempts at reforming the system and increasing efficiency have failed. For more than twenty years, cost containment has been a central concern of health-care professionals. For example, Congress enacted a system aimed at cost containment. This new system changed Medicare payments. Instead of paying hospitals a fee for services rendered, Medicare now pays hospitals a preset price for services based on an estimated cost of hospital care for patients in diagnostic related groups (DRG). This DRG system, while increasing efficiency and reducing the number of people in hospitals, seems to drive the sick into more outpatient care or critical care nursing homes. Despite this and other attempts at cost containment, overall health costs continue to rise.

So we are forced back to the difficult questions. Will there be enough resources? How do we determine who gets to use the available resources? Can we provide adequate care at an affordable price? Who shall live when not all can live?

Shaping a Response

Responses to such questions, of course, take different approaches. Some authors concentrate on the specific question of distributing scarce resources in situations involving a conflict of one life with another. For instance, if two people need a heart transplant but only one heart is available, who gets the heart? In this kind of case, experts generally suggest criteria with two stages. The first is medical acceptability: The only patients chosen are those who have some possibility of responding positively to the treatment. The second is the final selection from this first group. Formulating criteria for this final selection has proved to be very difficult. Such criteria as social worth or productivity (so the heart will go to the person who has done more for society) seem to deny the human dignity inherent in every person. Perhaps somewhat surprisingly, many authors settle on chance as the criterion for final selection. This randomness, whether lottery or simply "first come, first served," best respects human dignity by acknowledging an equal right to be saved.

Other authors begin by looking at different understandings of social justice as a way of determining who gets what care. Although the discussion remains very theoretical at this level, it alerts us to the pluralism of views in our society—views that may well shape policies and concrete health-care decisions. Here, for example, are five different understandings of justice: (1) to each according to his or her merit; (2) to each according to his or her contribution to society; (3) to each according to his or her free choice as a consumer; (4) to each according to his or her needs; (5) similar treatment for similar cases.

Obviously, which understanding of justice is used would have a profound impact on the distribution and use of medical resources.

While each view has its proponents, the discerning methodology presented in this book would reject the first three interpretations because they fail to respect the dignity of each individual. In the first, although many areas of health care do demand individual responsibility, people often face health crises beyond their control. Thus, merit is not an appropriate factor for determining health care. In the second, the worth of a human being cannot be determined by one's productivity in society. Also, the selection and ranking of criteria in a fair manner would prove impossible. In the third, selecting from a variety of competing goods will not work in the medical setting. When faced with life-or-death choices, an individual does not consider whether to purchase medical care or a new car. Free-market thinking, where one selects one's own values, breaks down in the face of urgent health needs.

The fourth and fifth positions do offer some helpful direction, although some nuancing and some additions are necessary. In the fourth, needs must be qualified as essential needs. Mere personal desires are not sufficient. In the fifth, a positive interpretation of similar treatment is required; impartially providing no treatment is not acceptable. The addition would come from a richer understanding of social justice as given in the Catholic tradition. We will return to this topic shortly.

These theoretical approaches to justice and especially the need for additions even in the acceptable interpretations point to an even deeper issue. A number of experts have emphasized the failure of cost-containment measures and have urged that the nation begin a realistic discussion concerning the rationing of resources. As part of this discussion, Daniel Callahan, the director of the Hastings Center, which is devoted to studying medical-moral issues, has pointed to the need for altering fundamental national convictions in order to address the health-care issues.

Specifically, Callahan focuses on such basic American values as individualism, openness to pluralism, trust in technology and suspicion of limits and government intervention. All these convictions move in a direction contrary to the difficult facts of the contemporary health-care crisis, contrary to the demands of rationing. Even the more theoretical approaches to justice emphasize self-interest and individualism.

The result is that we as a people tend to forget our interdependence and social connectedness. It is the community dimension, a sense of the common good, that Callahan and others judge to be the necessary foundation for responding to the crisis. Only this appreciation of the human community, which would represent a most significant change in our basic values, can ground the mutual help, mutual sacrifice and mutual limits involved in rationing. Such a switch in values still needs to be embodied in policies. These authors argue, however, that this new direction offers the only real chance of success, the only way to confront the reality that we cannot have everything we want, the only way to transform the health-care system before it collapses.

Catholic Tradition and the Common Good

It is especially at this point that a discerning methodology rooted in the Christian tradition can contribute to this dialogue. The Catholic tradition has developed a finely tuned sense of justice (detailed in the next chapter) which stresses the common good. Here the tradition can enlighten our American heritage, moving us beyond mere protection of individual rights to appreciation of the person as a social being with obligations to aid people in need and to create institutions that promote genuine mutuality and reciprocal respect.

Managed Care

The response to concerns about costs and resources that has in fact developed has been managed care. Although many different forms of managed care exist (for a very brief summary, see William Byron's article "Catholic Health Care: Partnering and Progress"), the basic idea is that someone coordinates and exercises oversight of health care. For example, an individual patient has a primary-care physician who oversees the person's care, including access to specialists. Similarly, the managed-care organization oversees what types of treatment the physicians in the organization are providing and at what cost.

In the former system of health care ("fee-for-service"), a patient paid usually through some form of insurance for the desired or needed treatment. Built into such a system was the temptation to do more than was necessary or helpful and to use the newest, fanciest technology. With managed care the temptation may be the opposite, because in some systems bonuses are paid to physicians whose treatment costs are less than expected (thus, by ordering certain expensive diagnostic tests, physicians may be reducing their own income).

The fears and ethical issues concerning managed care focus especially on the relationships between the patient and the physician and between the physician and the organization. First, because of the frequent change of health-care programs as employers look for the best deal, individuals may not be able to develop a relationship of trust and knowledge with a physician. Second, the pressure to reduce costs, even to the point of a physician not telling the patient about possible treatment options, may influence and even jeopardize the physician's care for patients; certainly there is the potential for a serious conflict of interest. Third, the organization's directives and guidelines for treatment may limit the kind and time of the physician's care. (One proposal that caused much public outrage, for example, was that mastectomies be done on an outpatient basis.)

Managed care, then, raises complex ethical dilemmas overlapping both medical ethics and business ethics. In his address "Managing Managed Care," Cardinal Joseph Bernardin, only several months before his death, provided a solid basis for ethical reflection on managed care at this time.

Bernardin places his discussion in the context of the consistent ethic of life (more on this topic in chapter six). This moral framework stresses that human life is sacred and so must be protected and respected from conception to death. Based on this foundation, Bernardin's view of health care emphasizes a number of points: (1) Health care is a service to persons in need, not just a commodity exchanged for profit; (2) health care must serve not only the individual but also the common good; (3) the needs of the poor have special priority; (4) limited resources must be managed realistically and wisely.

Managed care, according to Bernardin, can promote these health-care values—if managed properly! Managed care often emphasizes preventive health care, has the potential for dealing with the rationing of resources, and so achieves the broadest possible coverage of the nation's population. (Bernardin prefers to call this rationing stewardship: "How do we best protect human life and enhance human dignity in a situation of limited health resources?")

Bernardin also acknowledges the real and potential problems of managed care, that is, the undermining of health-care values. Many of these problems are rooted in economics. For example, managed-care plans may try to limit their enrollment to healthier populations (to reduce risk). Compensation, incentives and practice guidelines may lead to limited access to needed services. The consolidation of health-care services into networks may threaten the independence of health-care institutions (especially religiously affiliated ones with their special care for the poor).

Seeing both promise and peril, Bernardin urges dialogue and vigilance. Without them, he states, we "could find that economic goals supplant health goals."

In its statement "Ethical Issues in Managed Care," the Council on Ethical and Judicial Affairs of the American Medical Association expresses many similar concerns and cautions. The Council offers a number of guidelines to protect the patient-physician relationship, including the point that patients must thoroughly understand the terms of their health-care plans. The signs of the times, then, indicate that managed care—along with the larger issue of scarce resources—will remain for some time a debated and difficult ethical dilemma.

CATECHISM REFERENCES

Nos. 2273–2301, 2357–2359, 2375–2379, 2464–2499, 2534–2557.

FOR REFLECTION AND DISCUSSION

1. The stem-cell debate can become very emotional. How might your personal or family experience influence your moral reflections? What about the influence of movie and TV stars? What role ought the government play? Why?

2. The Catholic church has consistently opposed euthanasia, but official teaching has not stated a definite position on sustaining life-support systems. How can one be sure that withdrawing such support is done for the good of the patient rather than because of personal unwillingness to accept pain and sacrifice? How have you or someone you know made such a decision? Applying the discerning method developed in the first three chapters, what decision do you reach in the Brophy and Conroy cases?

3. Why is the distinction between killing and allowing to die significant? We try to live as faithful disciples of Jesus and as committed citizens; we also remember that what is legal may not be moral. If euthanasia and assisted suicide are legalized, what can you do to nourish and hand on the Christian tradition of respect for life in your family and parish? How can you get involved in the discussion about public policy?

4. Have you anticipated the possibility of one day needing life-support systems? Have you discussed with your family your desires concerning treatment? Have you investigated the living will and the durable power of attorney for health care? (These are ways to provide for decision-making when you are no longer able; for more information, check with your doctor or lawyer.)

5. What do you know about AIDS? Do you feel fear or prejudice against persons with AIDS? Do you know anyone with AIDS? Read *The Many Faces of AIDS* and *Called to Compassion and Responsibility*. How do these documents help you appreciate the profound medical and moral dilemmas related to AIDS? What local organizations or agencies might you contact if you want to volunteer some time responding to this crisis?

6. The scarcity of resources is a massive problem. Have you (or someone you know) experienced the limits imposed by managed care? What are your reactions to the call for rationing? What needs to be done to foster a sense of the common good, to move from individualism to mutual help? How can this be expressed in public policy? In your local community, what can you do?

chapter six

S O C I A L   E T H I C S

National and international problems at times seem overwhelming. In our newspapers and on TV, we are confronted with wars and violence, starvation and oppression, racism and terrorism. Situations appear to be desperate; solutions impossible. We ourselves are tempted to yield to despair or to escape to numbness. The issues, of course, do not go away. Through its teachings, the church has attempted to respond to them, offering guidance according to gospel values and urging individual and community participation in reforming the institutions and structures of society.

In this chapter we will first review the social teachings of the Catholic church and their application to life in the United States, then focus on the American pastoral letters on war and peace and on the economy, and conclude with the moral framework that holds all these issues together—the consistent ethic of life.

Dramatic world events—the breakup of the Soviet Union, the collapse of communism, the terrorism of 9/11 and the violent U.S. response—have emphasized the relevance of these social ethics. Although the end of the Cold War as we have experienced it allowed us to step back from the edge of nuclear destruction, the tragic experiences of genocide, regional wars, the possibility of chemical warfare, and especially terrorism and the wars in Afghanistan and Iraq all point to the urgency of ending violence and building a world of justice and peace. At the same time, economic issues have become even more pressing, both as the gap between rich and poor nations becomes greater and as more countries turn to some form of capitalism for solutions. This review, then, serves two purposes: (1) It covers major social problems that the world has faced for many years; (2) it presents key aspects of the church's positions regarding these issues.

THE SOCIAL TEACHINGS OF THE CHURCH

As its history of almsgiving and of founding hospitals and orphanages clearly indicates, the church has always been concerned for those in need. Pope Leo XIII's 1891 encyclical, *The Condition of Labor* (*Rerum Novarum*), written in response to the massive changes in society resulting from the industrial revolution, marks the beginning of the modern tradition of concern for social issues.

This tradition, expressed primarily in documents from popes, Vatican II and national conferences of bishops, stresses social justice and human dignity.

The church's social teachings are based on the traditional division of justice: commutative (relating to contractual obligations between individuals); distributive (dealing with society's relationship with individuals, distributing the benefits and burdens of societal life); and social (concerning the individual's responsibility to society). Social justice, then, has as its objective the service of the common good. The common good, as Blessed Pope John XXIII described it in his 1961 encyclical *Christianity and Social Progress* (*Mater et Magistra*), includes all those conditions of society that enable people more fully to achieve their own perfection as human beings.

This whole concept of justice is itself rooted in the Christian understanding of the person. This Christian anthropology, with its emphasis on human dignity because we are created in God's image and brought to abundant life in Jesus, grounds all the social teachings. It is most clearly expressed in Vatican II's *Church in the Modern World* (as we saw in chapter one). With this foundation of human dignity and social justice, the Catholic tradition has been able to address the urgent social problems of the past century.

LEO XIII's *THE CONDITION OF LABOR*

In 1891 the critical issue was industrialization and the oppression of workers, including child labor, long workdays and terrible working conditions. In response Pope Leo applied his understanding of human dignity and justice. Specifically, he claimed that this dignity is best protected by the right to work, the right to receive a just wage, the right to be respected as a person, the right to form unions and the right to private property.

Since each person has the duty to preserve his or her life, Leo argued, then each person has a right to the means necessary to life, that is, to work and thus secure necessities. This implies a just wage. Leo says that a worker must not be forced through fear to accept less (a common problem at that stage of industrialization). A forced contract clearly violates justice. The worker is to be respected as a human being, not treated as a slave. Working conditions should not degrade the person; neither should the worker be sacrificed for financial gain.

Leo went on to defend the right of workers to form unions. He considered organizing to improve conditions and to protect individuals a natural human right. Governments must protect natural rights, not destroy them. A government that would not allow the existence of unions is contradicting itself.

The Condition of Labor places much emphasis on the right to private property as a defense for human dignity. Human beings not only enjoy the goods of the earth but also choose and plan for the future. Leo stated that the obligations of family life—to provide the necessities of life and to protect against uncertainties—are best met by privately owned goods. He deplored the oppression and greed of unrestricted capitalism, and he strongly reacted against socialism because of its message of class conflict and denial of private property.

PIUS XI'S LETTERS

Economic and labor issues were still the focus of concern in 1931. Depression had worldwide impact, and Pope Pius XI responded to this situation in *The Reconstruction of the Social Order (Quadragesimo Anno)*.

Pius reaffirmed much of Leo's thought, backing unions and just wages and condemning unequal distribution of wealth. He also supported private property but emphasized its social dimension. Although the individual has a right to private property, its use must be in terms of the common good, for the goods of the earth are for all people. Like Leo, Pius strongly opposed unrestricted capitalism because it ignores the common good and oppresses the worker. Pius also condemned Marxism because of its atheism, materialism and promotion of class conflict.

Finally, *The Reconstruction of the Social Order* recommends the reconstruction of society by means of "corporatism," functional labor-management groups based on medieval guilds. These groups provide structures of economic self-government. Pius intends them to break down divisions between workers and owners, to increase distribution of property, to reduce antagonism between social classes and so to serve as a corrective to the injustices of capitalism and communism.

Attention, however, quickly turned to issues of war. In two 1937 encyclicals, Pius XI opposed the denial of human rights by Nazism and by Soviet Communism. Later, during World War II, his successor Pius XII used his Christmas broadcasts to emphasize human dignity and rights, particularly in the social and political fields.

JOHN XXIII AND HUMAN RIGHTS

After the war the focus briefly returned to economic issues, although with new emphasis on global interdependence and on the vast differences between rich and poor nations. John XXIII's 1961 *Christianity and Social Progress* (*Mater et Magistra*) addressed growing economic complexities. John used more modern concepts, recommending worker participation and collective bargaining in place of Pius XI's corporatism. He expressed concern not only for the industrial worker but also for the farmer.

This developing body of Catholic social thought still had its limits, however. From the time of the French Revolution, the Catholic Church was hesitant about some individual rights. In reaction to anticlericalism and the secularization of society, some popes moved from caution to actual hostility and condemnation of such rights. It was not until 1963 and John XXIII's *Peace on Earth* (*Pacem in Terris*) that democracy and individual rights of speech and religion were affirmed. This encyclical is an important declaration of human dignity, justice and rights. It deserves careful analysis.

The goal of John's document is peace; the foundation for this goal is human dignity. The encyclical affirms that all people are equal in nature, nobility and dignity. Based directly on this human nature are universal and inalienable rights. Recognition of and respect for both the person's dignity and these universal rights is the only sure foundation for a just and peaceful world. John adds that viewing human dignity from the perspective of revelation greatly increases our appreciation of this reality. In fact, however, *Peace on Earth* emphasizes human nature rather than revelation.

Human dignity is always present in the person; it is not bestowed by family or society or government. Instead, human dignity makes a claim on other persons and on society. For this dignity to be realized in particular historical and cultural settings, specific forms of behavior and social structures are required. These specific demands of human dignity are called rights. Rights, then, are values that are the necessary conditions for the realization of the basic value, human dignity.

Pope John goes on to consider some of these fundamental rights. The first is simply the right to life itself and to the means necessary for the proper development of life. Included are basics such as food, clothing and shelter, but also needed for the proper development of life are the right to seek truth and to express one's ideas, the right to worship God according to one's conscience and the right to be protected by law. Among social, economic and political rights, John lists the right to free assembly and association, the right to education, the right to choose one's vocation, the right to take an active part in public affairs, the right to a just wage and the right to private property.

Corresponding to these rights are responsibilities and duties. *Peace on Earth* gives an example of this reciprocity: With the right of every person to life comes the duty to preserve it. Such reciprocity is also found on the level of society. To one person's right there corresponds the duty of others to respect that right. Clearly, such a situation offers the potential for much conflict.

So John attempts to apply his view of human dignity and rights to issues of government. One of the chief concerns of civil authorities is the defense and promotion of personal rights, the maintenance of the proper balance of individuals' rights and duties. Justice requires not only respect for rights but also fulfillment of duties. When rights conflict, John urges that disputes be settled in a way worthy of human dignity and not by force. Governments must be willing to work together, to cooperate in seeking economic and social progress. John especially condemns the arms race because vast amounts of intellectual and economic resources are directed away from the development of nations to the increase of armaments. The relationship between governments must be based on freedom. Only this freedom fully respects the rights and dignity of other peoples.

Particularly important in this context of international cooperation is the concept of the common good. John argues that in today's world the common good of one nation cannot be separated from the common good of the whole human family. John encourages economically developed nations to aid those in the process of development so that every person may live in conditions in keeping with human dignity. John also warns powerful nations to respect the freedom of poor nations. In giving economic aid, wealthy nations must not seek cultural and political domination. Finally, John expresses his concern about the universal common good, recognizing the grave and complex problems concerning world peace. Since such worldwide problems can only be met by some form of worldwide authority, John turns in hope to the United Nations as a protector of human rights and dignity.

Peace on Earth is clearly a bold declaration of human dignity and rights, a comprehensive statement that moves from the individual to the entire human family.

While many of John's themes were continued and expanded by later social teachings, a fundamental change was soon introduced. Even as *Peace on Earth* was written, Vatican II was opening the windows of renewal in the church. A major aspect of this renewal was the return to Scripture. From this time on, social teachings would emphasize scriptural views of the human rather than the more philosophical natural law tradition. As we saw in chapter one, Vatican II's *The Church in the Modern World* clearly exemplifies this change. This document still stresses human dignity as the basis for responses to the urgent issues of today's world but now grounds this dignity in revelation. Scripture teaches that the human being is created in God's image, can know and love the Creator and is created for interpersonal communion. Human beings are also sinners. In Jesus Christ sin is overcome, and the person's full dignity and destiny is revealed. Vatican II uses this view of human dignity to suggest particular responses to some critical issues: marriage and family; the proper development of culture; social, economic and political life; war and peace.

PAUL VI AND HUMAN DEVELOPMENT

Pope Paul VI also spoke out against the vast differences between nations. More and more he stressed the social dimension of property. His 1967 encyclical, *The Development of Peoples* (*Populorum Progressio*), takes a firm stand: "Private property does not constitute for anyone an absolute and unconditioned right. No one is justified in keeping for his exclusive use what he does not need, when others lack necessities" (23). Paul emphasizes a deeper meaning of development, stating that the needs of the whole person—cultural, social, religious—must be considered, not just economic concerns. He urges fair trade relations and other forms of international cooperation.

Paul's 1971 *A Call to Action* (*Octogesima Adveniens*) also condemns flagrant inequalities existing in the cultural, economic and political development of nations, focusing on political power. The goal of such power must be the common good, respecting individual rights and creating conditions that help the individual lead a truly human life. Paul discusses other social justice issues: urbanization, discrimination, the environment and the role of women. He also highlights the role of individual Christians and local churches in responding to injustices.

Also in 1971, the Synod of Bishops (several hundred bishops representing the bishops of the whole church) called justice a constitutive (that is, essential) element of the gospel and of the church's mission. The Synod's statement, *Justice in the World*, opposes the divisions between rich and poor that leave millions of people illiterate, ill-fed and ill-housed, lacking human responsibility and dignity.

The document shows how the church's mission of liberation is rooted in Scripture. According to the gospel, one's relationship with God is closely akin to one's relationships with other persons. To love God is to love one's neighbor. This love of neighbor cannot exist without justice, a recognition of the individual's dignity and rights. The recommendations of the Synod for promoting justice focus on human dignity and rights: respect for rights within the church itself; an examination of conscience concerning one's lifestyle; education to overcome materialism and individualism; ecumenical cooperation on religious liberty; international action to recognize and protect inalienable human rights and dignity as expressed in the United Nations' *Universal Declaration of Human Rights*.

Both of these 1971 documents discuss two themes that have received greater priority in recent years: the preferential option for the poor and the reform of society to enable all persons to participate fully in their society's economic, political and cultural life.

John Paul II's Teachings

Pope John Paul II continued the social teaching tradition with his encyclicals, especially *On Human Work (Laborem Exercens)* (1981), *On Social Concern (Sollicitudo Rei Socialis)* (1987), and *On the Hundredth Anniversary of Rerum Novarum (Centesimus Annus)* (1991). *On Human Work* commemorates the ninetieth anniversary of Leo XIII's *The Condition of Labor* and again supports the rights of workers and unions. John Paul focuses on work, stressing that work expresses and increases human dignity and contributes to the common good. John Paul not only addresses the issue of technology by emphasizing the primacy of people over things, he also discusses the influence and views of various ideologies. John Paul criticizes Marxism with its emphasis on collectivism and its rejection of private property. He criticizes capitalism for its neglect of the common good, materialism for its subordination of spiritual aspects of life to material things. John Paul promotes systems (joint ownership, shareholding by labor and so on) that reconcile capital and labor. He concludes his reflections with some thoughts on a spirituality of work. Through work people share in the wonder of creation and participate in the paschal mystery. Work includes toil and the cross but also great grace, allowing people to fulfill their vocation as human beings.

On Social Concern commemorates the twentieth anniversary of *The Development of Peoples*. John Paul reaffirms the continuity of the church's social teaching as well as its ongoing renewal. He reflects on the central theme of Paul VI's encyclical, the development of peoples, in light of current signs of the times.

In fact, John Paul judges, the reality of the developing nations has become worse. Earlier hopes for development are far from being realized. Many societies today are characterized by underdevelopment—not only economic but also cultural, political and human underdevelopment. John Paul sees the massive economic gap between the north and south hemispheres rooted in the ideological differences between East and West. And so he urges genuine dialogue and collaboration for peace so that resources and investments now devoted to arms production can be redirected to relieving impoverished peoples. John Paul reaffirms the richer and more authentic sense of human development, including all dimensions of the fully human. Finally he addresses sinful structures, which are rooted in personal sin and so linked to concrete acts of the individuals who form and consolidate these structures. The path to overcome this moral evil is long and complex. It is the path of conversion, of solidarity, of the graced commitment to the common good.

On the Hundredth Anniversary of Rerum Novarum celebrates one hundred years of social teachings by reaffirming that this teaching is an essential part of evangelization. The encyclical begins by highlighting key themes from Leo XIII's encyclical—the dignity of persons, the rights of workers, private property understood in the context of the common good—and indicating how they remain valid for today's world. The encyclical also provides John Paul's first commentary on the effects of the collapse of communism in Eastern Europe, and so concentrates on economic issues. He states that the collapse was in part rooted in communism's atheistic view of humanity and in violation of workers' rights. Following the long tradition of the social teachings, the pope rejects a capitalism that is not limited by a strong legal framework, but recognizes a business economy that protects the dignity of people. While he acknowledges the benefits of a free market society, the pope adds a strong caution about consumerism, which harms both human beings and the environment. John Paul also condemns class conflict and discusses the proper role of government. He calls for a more just sharing of power and of all forms of property, including information and technology, and expresses his grave concern about growing poverty and marginalization.

Continuity and Change

This tradition of modern Catholic social teaching has clearly emphasized human dignity and justice. This dignity and the cluster of rights and duties related to it form the basis for the church's perspective on a whole range of social problems: industrialization, economic depression, unions, international trade, poverty, hunger, imperialism, Marxism, property, war and peace. The official teachings embody both continuity and change. They consistently appeal to human dignity as the basis of response to all these moral dilemmas.

Understanding and expressing this dignity develops, however, from a natural law perspective to a more scriptural one. Another fundamental transition is the change from viewing human dignity and social justice simply as concerns of the church (as expressed by Leo XIII) to the recognition that the defense of human dignity and the promotion of justice are essential elements of the church's mission (as expressed by the 1971 Synod).

Other constant themes throughout the years have been the defense of the rights of the working class and of labor unions, the condemnation of the gap between rich and poor and opposition to Marxism. Other changes include the movement from opposition to support of democracy and individual rights, the growing emphasis on the social dimension of private property and the recognition of valid state intervention.

Finally, three other aspects of the social teachings deserve to be highlighted:

1) There is a very close relationship between justice and love in the Catholic social tradition. Love of neighbor cannot exist without justice, but

justice cannot be fully realized without love. The tradition emphasizes love as the foundation of justice but also develops and applies a theory of justice (the distributive/commutative/social distinction described earlier) that provides structure and continuity, thereby avoiding appealing to a love ethic that does not specify rights and duties.

2) Throughout the modern Catholic social tradition, human dignity and rights are viewed in a personalist perspective, not an individualist one. The person is always understood as a social being, a view that implies social interdependence and mutual obligation and duty. This social awareness and the emphasis on the common good distinguishes the Catholic tradition from the natural rights tradition that shaped the United States Declaration of Independence and Bill of Rights. The Catholic tradition supports a positive responsibility to reach out to others in need. Respect for dignity, justice and freedom means not only not interfering with others' actions but also aiding people in need and contributing to the common good. In the United States tradition, justice and rights protect individuals from outside interference.

3) The social teachings demonstrate an appreciation of advancing human knowledge, an acceptance of change and a recognition of pluralism. Beginning with *The Condition of Labor*, the social teachings have attempted to read the signs of the times and to recognize the profound and rapid changes occurring in society. The natural sciences and especially the human sciences have played essential roles in understanding these changes and their implications for human life. In *A Call to Action* Paul VI describes the sciences as "a condition at once indispensable and inadequate for a better discovery of what is human." Also in that document he acknowledges the possibility of a variety of responses to specific issues.

Rooted in this kind of openness while at the same time consistently emphasizing human dignity and rights, the social teachings, especially since Vatican II, embody and express the key characteristics of a contemporary Catholic morality as described in the first three chapters of this book. While the natural law perspective is retained, recent documents stress their scriptural foundations. The social teachings exemplify a dialogue between the Christian tradition and contemporary insights and issues. The social teachings center on the person, a being in time who comes to full humanity only in relationship with others and through participation in particular political, economic, social and religious institutions.

POLITICAL RESPONSIBILITY

The papal and conciliar documents, which address the whole world, recognize the need to translate this sometimes abstract vision into the specifics of the local Christian community. The American bishops have attempted to apply the social teachings to life in the United States, in part through a great variety of documents. Until recently, the bishops gathered under the title of the National Conference of Catholic Bishops (NCCB). The NCCB had its historical roots in the National Catholic War Council (formed in 1917 after Cardinal James Gibbons of Baltimore promised President Woodrow Wilson that the Catholic church would cooperate in every possible way in the war effort) and the National Catholic Welfare Conference (formed after World War I to continue coordinating national efforts). This conference was reformed according to the directives of Vatican II and renamed the NCCB. Revisions in 2001 led to the new name and structure, the United States Conference of Catholic Bishops (USCCB).

Throughout their history, the conferences have responded to the major social issues of the country. Since 1976 the Administrative Board/Committee has issued a statement on political responsibility in connection with each United States presidential election. For 2004, the Committee presented its challenging document, *Faithful Citizenship: A Catholic Call to Political Responsibility.* The statement highlights some key concerns of the country and church, poses ten questions about human dignity and the common good, discusses the relationship between faith and politics, summarizes major themes of Catholic social teaching, and addresses four areas of national and global concern.

Faithful Citizenship includes a long list of earlier documents from the U.S. bishops, encouraging even more in-depth study of public policy issues. And, of course, it also directs attention back to the fundamental question: Will faithful citizens receive the statement as a reminder that the gospel is the basis of their political choices or will they read *Faithful Citizenship* through the lens of a political party or some other value? The bishops frequently imply this question, urging all "to see beyond party politics" and affirming that faithful citizenship "begins with moral principles not party platforms." And again: "Faithful citizenship calls Catholics to see civic and political responsibilities through the eyes of faith and to bring our moral convictions to public life."

Faithful Citizenship reaffirms the bishops' emphasis on a consistent moral framework for addressing all political, economic and social issues. The document collects dozens of these issues under four categories: protecting human life, promoting family life, pursuing social justice, practicing global solidarity. This call for consistency along with the highlighting of so many issues is particularly challenging. No one issue is sufficient to determine a political choice, and no one party is consistently pro-life. What is a voter to do?

The bishops acknowledge the dilemma. They write that "some Catholics may feel politically homeless sensing that no political party and too few candidates share a consistent concern for human life and dignity." Still, they go on to urge people to vote with an informed conscience and to get involved, reminding all that participation in the political process is a moral obligation.

Hard homework is necessary for an informed conscience. But it is so hard for people to take in and live gospel values. All receive so many messages that contradict the gospel—powerful messages from advertising, political parties, TV and films, newspapers, business, even families. The understanding of the meaning of life and reactions to events in the world often are rooted in these competing messages rather than in the Scriptures. For example, rather than follow Jesus' example of nonviolence, many people turn to violence to solve conflicts—as *Faithful Citizenship* states: Our nation turns to "abortion to deal with difficult pregnancies; the death penalty to combat crime; euthanasia and assisted suicide to deal with the burdens of age, illness and disability; and war to address international disputes."

The Catholic tradition's emphasis on solidarity with the whole human family, on special concern for the poor and vulnerable, on economic justice and the common good often distinguishes Catholic principles from the lived values in the U.S. culture and from elements of the platforms of both major political parties.

Recent years provide many examples of this conflict between the gospel vision of life and some U.S. social, economic or political practices. Some of these issues are found in the long list of concerns in *Faithful Citizenship:* (1) deadly violence of terror, war, starvation and children dying from disease, (2) abortion and euthanasia, (3) health care coverage for all, (4) nuclear arms and global trade in arms, (5) death penalty and the criminal justice system, (6) jobs and unions, (7) welfare reform, (8) protection of immigrants, (9) environmental concerns, (10) global poverty and underdevelopment.

Faithful Citizenship easily leads to the following reflection. What is *our* challenge as faithful disciples and as involved citizens in elections? Where do we even begin? First, we can examine our conscience and prayerfully reflect on our reactions to politics. Does the gospel or a particular political party shape our fundamental values and commitments? Second, we need to read carefully *Faithful Citizenship* and other sources of information, then discuss the issues with families and friends and parish and community members. Third, we must vote. This may not be as simple as it seems. The choice is usually not very clear, for the platforms and policies of all the political parties at times contradict the gospel vision of life.

Especially since often there is no clear match between the bishops' position and any of the candidates, prayerful discernment will be necessary. A possible process: Start by praying for God's guidance and wisdom in making your political choices. Read additional information, for example, some of the other statements listed in *Faithful Citizenship*. Continue discussions, trying to listen carefully to positions different from your own. Spend prayerful time with the image of the table described in the Introduction of the bishops' statement. Enter the table scene with an open and compassionate heart rather than preconceived ideas and answers. Take a week for each set of the ten questions. Pray, study, reflect, discuss. During this time, if possible, find some concrete action to perform that is connected with the table image or one of the questions. For example, volunteer in a shelter for the homeless or in an AIDS clinic. Keep in mind the haunting question of Scripture scholar Walter Wink: "How can we oppose evil without creating new evils and being made evil ourselves?" Pay attention in this whole process to that which best promotes the flourishing of all life. Then vote.

THE CHALLENGE OF PEACE

From *Faithful Citizenship* we now turn to a detailed look at two major pastoral letters and the urgent issues they address: *The Challenge of Peace* (1983) and *Economic Justice for All* (1986). These lengthy statements are significant both for their content and for their methodology. Each statement went through consultations, public debate and several drafts before the bishops approved the final version. This collaborative process clearly exemplifies an openness to a wide variety of expert judgments and an appropriate use of authority. Such a process fits well the demands of responding to contemporary moral dilemmas.

When the American bishops issued *The Challenge of Peace* in 1983, they were addressing the most pressing issue of the day, the possible destruction of the world. It was a supreme crisis; nuclear weapons threatened human life and human civilization. The bishops, speaking as moral teachers, not technical experts, tackled the complexities of war and peace in order to provide hope for all people and direction toward a world freed from the nuclear threat. They stated: "We are the first generation since Genesis with the power to virtually destroy God's creation. We cannot remain silent in the face of such danger. Why do we address these issues? We are simply trying to live up to the call of Jesus to be peacemakers in our own time and situation" (331).

The remarkable changes in the relationship between the United States and Russia, the superpowers, have calmed the crisis somewhat. Weapons have been destroyed, or at least directed away from cities toward oceans. Economic pressures limit massive increases of arms production. Nuclear weapons still exist, however; indeed, they are considered the cornerstone of the American deterrent strategy. Moreover, both terrorism and U.S. withdrawal from arms treaties and its desire for new nuclear arms create new threats. A careful consideration of *The Challenge of Peace*, then, remains a vital task for our day.

THE TRADITION, WAR AND PEACE

The bishops begin their pastoral letter by reviewing the Catholic teaching on war and peace. From the Hebrew Scriptures come such themes as peace as a gift of God's saving activity, peace as a special characteristic of the covenant (implying care for the needy and absolute trust in God), hope for a messianic time of justice and peace. In the New Testament the words and deeds of Jesus proclaim the reign of God, a new reality wonderfully described in the Sermon on the Mount. After his violent death, Jesus is raised as a sign that God does reign and does give life in death. To his followers Jesus gives the gift of peace and calls them to be peacemakers.

Peace, of course, has not yet been fully realized. Throughout history, people encounter personal sin and public violence. War has been an all-too-common reality. The Christian tradition has responded to this reality, expressing a strong presumption against war but acknowledging that this presumption can be overridden in order to protect human dignity and rights. This nuanced teaching is called the "just-war theory."

The theory dates back to Saint Augustine. (Note 31 in the pastoral letter gives references about the history and theology of the just-war tradition.) *The Challenge of Peace* presents both the conditions necessary for resorting to force and also the limits on using force. The decision to wage war is justified when: (1) There is a just cause (for example, to preserve conditions necessary for decent human existence); (2) the decision is made by those responsible for public order; (3) the rights and values involved justify killing; (4) there is a right intention, such as to protect rights and pursue peace; (5) all peaceful alternatives to war have been exhausted; (6) there is some probability of success (although defense of significant values even against great odds may be justified); (7) the damage and costs of the war are proportionate to the good expected.

Even when the decision to engage in war meets these criteria, two other criteria apply to the actual waging of war: proportionality and discrimination. These principles are particularly significant in light of the destructive potential of today's weapons. The bishops question whether limitation of war is possible, or whether escalation to total war may in fact occur. Clearly this possibility would be terribly disproportionate, for what value could justify the destruction of civilization? Likewise, just response to aggression must be discriminant, that is, directed against unjust aggressors but not innocent people caught up in the war. Total war would necessarily take many innocent lives, and so violate the principle of discrimination.

The bishops include another response to unjust aggression: nonviolence. Deeply embedded in the Christian tradition, nonviolence affirms the use of prayer and other nonviolent means of answering hostility. Christian pacifism is not passive about injustice but exemplifies what it means to resist injustice through nonviolent methods. (Nonviolence is stressed even more in *The Harvest of Justice Is Sown in Peace*, the U.S. bishops' reflection on peacemaking commemorating the tenth anniversary of *The Challenge of Peace*.)

SPECIFIC RECOMMENDATIONS

In light of this complex Christian tradition, the bishops interpret the signs of the times regarding the nuclear arms race. They stress the magnitude of destruction that would result from total war and acknowledge that restating general moral principles is not a sufficient response to this crisis. A more nuanced response must include examination of weapons systems, the policies that govern their use and the consequences of using them. Accordingly, *The Challenge of Peace* carefully discusses the use of nuclear weapons, the policy of deterrence in principle and in practice, specific steps to reduce the danger of war and long-term measures of policy and diplomacy.

Concerning the use of nuclear weapons, the bishops conclude that under no circumstances may nuclear weapons be used to destroy predominantly civilian targets. This judgment also applies to the retaliatory use of weapons against enemy cities. Because the difficulties of limiting the use of nuclear weapons are so great, the bishops state that they cannot imagine a situation that would justify the deliberate initiation of nuclear warfare. Finally, the bishops seriously question whether any kind of limited nuclear exchange is possible. The just-war criteria lead the bishops to conclude that the first imperative is to prevent any use of nuclear weapons.

Deterrence continues to be a much-debated topic. *The Challenge of Peace* uses this definition of deterrence: "dissuasion of a potential adversary from initiating an attack or conflict, often by the threat of unacceptable retaliatory damage" (163). Such deterrence has been at the center of both United States and Soviet policy. Some people say that deterrence has worked, since nuclear weapons have not been used since 1945. Others concentrate on the high risk of deterrence: What would be the result of just one failure? The bishops wrestle with this complex issue, along with United States policies and the direction provided by just-war criteria. They finally end with a "strictly conditioned moral acceptance of nuclear deterrence" (186). It is not, however, a long-term basis for peace but only a step on the way toward progressive disarmament.

The bishops add that they cannot approve every weapons system or policy recommended in the name of deterrence. Specifically, they reject plans for repeated nuclear strikes, first-strike weapons and the quest for nuclear superiority. They recommend agreements to stop the testing and production of new nuclear weapons systems, reduction of present arsenals and a comprehensive test ban treaty. Although the bishops do not condemn all aspects of nuclear deterrence, they emphasize their profound skepticism about the moral acceptability of any use of nuclear weapons. They urge, therefore, the revision of the United States policy on deterrence and the movement toward a more stable system of international security.

Quoting John Paul II, "Like a cathedral, peace must be constructed patiently and with unshakable faith" (200), the bishops offer steps to reduce the danger of war and to build peace. Of prime importance are efforts to achieve arms control and mutual disarmament, ratification of treaties, negotiations to reduce political tensions around the world and the development of nonviolent methods of conflict resolution.

Recognition of global interdependence is the foundation for a positive conception of peace. The human family is a unity with shared bonds of rights and duties. Problems and conflicts are also shared on a global scale, so that mutual security and even survival demand a new appreciation of interdependence. In this context, the bishops address the superpowers, the United States and the Soviet Union. Acknowledging vast differences, the bishops also stress the urgent practical need for cooperation. Political dialogue and negotiations must be pursued with a certain openness so that changes in ideologies and relationships are possible. Also in this context of interdependence, the bishops discuss complex economic issues, especially the growing chasm between rich and poor nations. Meeting economic needs is an essential element for a peaceful world. The impact of the arms race is highlighted here, as the letter cites *The Church in the Modern World*: "The arms race is one of the greatest curses on the human race and the harm it inflicts upon the poor is more than can be endured" (269). Only if the spending on arms is reversed will there be sufficient resources for many human needs around the world. The bishops claim that the political will to redirect scientific and technological capacity to meet these needs is part of the challenge of the nuclear age.

The bishops conclude their long pastoral letter by reminding Christians that to be faithful to their call may mean taking a stand against commonly held positions. Discipleship certainly includes a reverence for life. "When we accept violence, war itself can be taken for granted. Violence has many faces: oppression of the poor, deprivation of basic human rights, economic exploitation, sexual exploitation and pornography, neglect or abuse of the aged and the helpless, and innumerable other acts of inhumanity. Abortion in particular blunts a sense of the sacredness of human life" (285). The bishops agree with Paul VI: "If you wish peace, defend life" (289). The bishops end with words of challenge and hope, confident in God's presence and action in our world.

NEW THREATS

The 9/11 terrorist attacks on New York and Washington D.C., followed by the violent U.S. responses have created new threats to world peace. Not surprisingly, the terrorism evoked different responses, from calling for immediate retaliation and vengeance to urging a police action and the use of international courts to appealing for long-term efforts to reduce the causes of terrorism. Various sides justified their position by using the just-war theory.

A remarkable perspective was also offered by the liturgical readings. The liturgical calendar, of course, had long been established. It was, then, merely coincidence that, immediately after the attacks of 9/11, the church was proclaiming Luke's Sermon on the Plain during weekday liturgies. The texts included these excerpts: "Blessed are you who weep now, for you will laugh" (Luke 6:21) and "But I say to you that listen, Love your enemies, do good to those who hate you, bless those who curse you, pray for those who abuse you" (Luke 6:27, 28).

Surely God's word has much to say to people as they try to respond as faithful disciples of Jesus to world events. Jesus often offers a vision very different from what they usually hear from politicians and the media. He proclaims God's loving presence, inviting all to live with trust, compassion, nonviolence and love.

Jesus' vision inspired U.S. Jesuits working in Peru to write to President George W. Bush. Given not only their faith but also their direct experience of terrorism over many years (parishes bombed, at least one of them captured by the Shining Path terrorists, much death and horror throughout Peru), they wanted to share the wisdom of their experience with the president. They wrote:

> Here in Peru it took us a long time to learn about the nature of terrorism and to find effective ways to struggle against it. We do not want the people of our native land to have to endure the same struggle of trial and error. We do not want our fellow countrymen and women to fall into the same trap of the vicious circle of violence breeding more violence . . . .
>
> Only when the terrorists could not demand support from the villagers did their campaign begin to decline. On the other hand, when the police and armed forces themselves

used their military might for direct attacks against the terrorists in the rural communities, they created a situation which made the terrorists appear to be the better alternative.

Terrorism is bred by ideological means, and it finds its ultimate justification in the poverty of the people who have no hope for a better life. Therefore, terrorism must be attacked on those same levels—by offering another "ideology" to counteract the terrorist system and by responding to the root causes of violence.

The U.S. leaders, however, chose to attack Afghanistan for harboring Osama bin Laden and his al-Qaida supporters. Debate, division and death followed. A number of U.S. bishops quickly concluded that it was a just war. Bishops from other parts of the world judged differently. Scholars discussed whether just-war theory had become useless or simply was not seriously applied.

It was in this context that John Paul II issued his message for World Peace Day on January 1, 2002. Inviting all people to begin the New Year with an urgent prayer for peace, the pope called for a deeper understanding of peace. His title, "No Peace Without Justice, No Justice Without Forgiveness," accurately indicates the heart of the pope's challenging message. He writes,

> I have often paused to reflect on the persistent question: how do we restore the moral and social order subjected to such horrific violence? My reasoned conviction, confirmed in turn by biblical revelation, is that the shattered order cannot be fully restored except by a response that combines justice with forgiveness. The pillars of true peace are justice and that form of love which is forgiveness.

The pope presents a sober analysis of the violence caused by organized terrorism, including the impact on the marginalized peoples in the developing world. He affirms the right to defend against terrorism, as long as this right is exercised in a legal and moral way. He also looks to the roots of terrorism: "International cooperation in the fight against terrorist activities must also include a courageous and resolute political, diplomatic and economic commitment to relieving situations of oppression and marginalization which facilitate the designs of terrorists."

As if anticipating people's rejection of the possibility of forgiveness, John Paul states,

> Forgiveness is not a proposal that can be immediately understood or easily accepted; in many ways it is a paradoxical message. Forgiveness, in fact, always involves an apparent short-term loss for a real long-term gain. Violence is the exact opposite; opting as it does for an apparent short-term gain, it involves a real and permanent loss. Forgiveness may seem like weakness, but it demands great spiritual strength and moral courage, both in granting it and in accepting it.

Pope John Paul's vision of peace was not a popular one. For many people, the first and still dominant instinct, supported by political leaders and the media, has been to wave the flag and drop the bombs. However, authentic peace, as John Paul indicates, only comes with justice and forgiveness. "No peace without justice, no justice without forgiveness: I shall not tire of repeating this warning to those who, for one reason or another, nourish feelings of hatred, a desire for revenge or the will to destroy."

Attention soon turned from Afghanistan to Iraq. As pressures for war increased, the U.S. bishops questioned the Bush Administration. In their November 2002 "Statement on Iraq" the bishops wrote: "Based on the facts that are known to us, we continue to find it difficult to justify the resort to war against Iraq....With the Holy See and bishops from the Middle East and around the world, we fear that the resort to war...would not meet the strict conditions in Catholic teaching for overriding the strong presumption against the use of military force."

On this issue of war against Iraq, there really was a great difference between political and religious leaders. Because so much of the U.S. media seemed to be hyping the war, perhaps many people were not aware of Pope John Paul's consistent opposition. In his address to the Diplomatic Corps, for example, the pope said; "War is not always inevitable. It is always a defeat for humanity." Solutions in the Middle East "will never be imposed by recourse to terrorism or armed conflict, as if military victories could be the solution." Vatican observers noted that John Paul II's gradual move toward limited use of just war was not unlike his move toward limited use of capital punishment—a possibility in theory, but rarely warranted in practice.

The Vatican addressed the United Nations with these words: "On the issue of Iraq, the vast majority of the international community is calling for a diplomatic resolution of the dispute and for exploring all avenues for a peaceful settlement. That call should not be ignored." Other Vatican officials commented that provision for preventive war is found neither in the *Catechism* nor in the United Nations Charter.

Still, polls showed that U.S. Catholics were in favor of a unilateral assault on Iraq by a margin of two to one. The Bush Administration, indeed, chose to pursue the path of a preemptive war.

How is it that the world's bishops disagreed about the war in Afghanistan or that so many U.S. Catholics chose to follow the president rather than the pope? The thought of Karl Rahner, s.j., may help answer these questions. In his *Theological Investigations XVIII,* Rahner points to what he calls "global prescientific convictions"—that is, unexamined assumptions, mostly cultural in character, that shape moral perceptions and analyses. These prejudgments mold people's moral imaginations and perceptions of basic values, sometimes making it difficult to live gospel values. Everyone receives many messages that contradict the gospel, from media and politics, business and families. One's vision of life and responses to world events often are based on these values rather than on the Scriptures and Christian tradition.

Perhaps that explains the post–9/11 reactions of so many people. Patriotism had slipped over into nationalism. The rhetoric of media and politicians was more convincing than the Sermon on the Mount. Vengeance triumphed over forgiveness and love of enemies. The very old religion of ancient Babylon that believes violence saves appeared as the real religion of the contemporary United States.

In contrast to violence saves, Jesus teaches that God saves. In his life and teaching, Jesus expresses his vision of the reign of God. In Jesus' vision, nonviolence is not passivity. Contemporary Scripture scholars have emphasized this distinction. "Turning the other cheek" (Matthew 5:38–42) is really about creative, nonviolent resistance, an action designed to protest oppression in the context of Roman occupation in the first century.

Many people are tempted to dismiss creative, nonviolent resistance to evil as idealistic and finally futile. History shows, however, that it does work, as in the Philippines, Poland and many other places. (For more on the religion of violence saves and on nonviolent resistance, see Walter Wink's *Engaging the Powers*.)

ECONOMIC JUSTICE FOR ALL

The bishops introduce *Economic Justice for All* with the claim that economic life is one of the chief areas where people live out their faith, love their neighbor and fulfill God's creative design. Economic decisions affect the quality of people's lives, even to the point of determining whether people live or die. The bishops note that they are pastors and moral teachers, not economists. Their purpose is not to suggest a particular economic theory but to attend to the human and ethical dimension of economic life and to invite new choices and new actions in pursuing economic justice.

The pastoral begins with three simple yet profound questions: "What does the economy do for people? What does it do to people? And how do people participate in it?" Looking at national and international realities, the bishops find both positive and negative answers to these questions. The nation can boast of the strength, productivity and creativity of its economy. Yet there exist many ugly realities too: homelessness and unemployment in the United States, poverty and starvation in many parts of the world.

THE BIBLICAL VISION

In response to these massive problems, the bishops offer a Christian vision of the economic life. The basic criterion against which all aspects of economic life must be measured is the dignity of the person along with the community and solidarity that are essential to this dignity. *Economic Justice for All* first turns to the Scriptures for developing the specifics of this sacredness of human beings, and then spells out familiar social justice themes of rights, duties and the common good.

From the Hebrew Scriptures the bishops take three fundamental themes that help people more fully understand who they are: creation, covenant and community. In Genesis we learn that God is Creator of heaven and earth and that creation is very good. At its summit stands the creation of man and woman, made in the image of God. So every human has an inalienable dignity. Everyone must also help care for creation, to be a faithful steward of this great gift. In this way people share in the creative activity of God. Genesis goes on to describe sin and alienation from God and others.

God, however, remains faithful. Exodus tells us the story of the Hebrews' deliverance. God frees the people and chooses them. In chapter one we have already reflected on this marvelous story of covenant and community. Faithfulness to the covenant was spelled out in the laws. Again and again the prophets called the people back to the covenant, demanding special concern for the vulnerable members of the community—widows, orphans, the poor and strangers in the land.

This tradition, of course, is Jesus' tradition. Jesus enters human history and announces the nearness of God's reign. As we saw in chapter one, Jesus himself embodies characteristics of life in God's reign: commitment, intimacy, care for the poor and outcast, trust, forgiveness, faithful action. Jesus invites his followers to a life of discipleship, patterning their lives on his.

In developing the theme of discipleship, *Economic Justice for All* explains the contemporary phrase, "preferential option for the poor." The bishops point out that in the New Testament salvation is extended to all people. At the same time, Jesus takes the side of those most in need, physically and spiritually. The parable of the rich man and the poor Lazarus (Luke 16:19–31) is just one example of many in the Gospels that direct attention to the dangers of wealth. The rich are easily blinded by wealth and tempted to make it into an idol. While material poverty is certainly not a good, the poor experience a dependence and powerlessness that may allow them more easily to be open to God's presence and power. Contemporary followers of Jesus, then, are challenged to take on this perspective: to see things from the side of the poor, to assess lifestyle and public policies in terms of their impact on the poor, to experience God's power in the midst of poverty and powerlessness.

MORAL ISSUES

Building not only on this biblical vision but also on the rich tradition of Catholic life and thought and on respect for the person and the demands of social justice, the bishops highlight six basic moral principles to help guide economic choices and shape economic institutions:

1) Every economic institution must be judged in light of whether it protects or undermines human dignity.

2) Human dignity can be realized only in community.

3) All people have a right to participate in the economic life of society.

4) All people have a special obligation to the poor

5) Human rights are the minimum conditions for life in community.

6) Society as a whole has the moral responsibility to enhance human dignity and protect human rights.

These principles ground the bishops' recommendations and challenges regarding economic justice.

After addressing various rights and duties of working people and unions, of owners and managers, of citizens and government, *Economic Justice for All* turns to four major economic issues: employment, poverty, agriculture and global interdependence. As the bishops move to these specific areas, they note several cautions:

- The pastoral letter is not a comprehensive analysis of the United States economy. It is an attempt to encourage moral analysis leading to a more just economy.

- Moral values do not dictate specific solutions. They help direct decisions, which must also take into account historical, social and political realities.

- Therefore the letter's recommendations do not carry the same authority as the statements on moral principles. These recommendations are to be taken seriously, but dialogue is expected.

The bishops state that full employment is the foundation of a just economy. Creation of new jobs with adequate pay and decent working conditions is therefore an urgent priority. For most people employment is crucial for self-realization and the fulfillment of material needs. The bishops go on to discuss the disastrous impact joblessness has on human lives and human dignity, the changes resulting from new technology and the continuing problem of discrimination in employment. They recommend a number of steps for both private and public sectors, including job training and apprenticeship programs and direct job-creation programs.

About one in every seven people in the United States is poor. While some move in and out of poverty, others remain poor for extended periods of time. Studies show that long-term poverty is concentrated among racial minorities and families headed by women. It is more likely to be found in rural areas and in the South. Most long-term poor are working for wages too low to bring them above poverty or are retired or disabled. Most are not able to work more hours than they already do. Poverty in our nation presents a great challenge: to develop a society where no one goes without the material resources necessary for human dignity and growth. *Economic Justice for All* discusses the very uneven distribution of wealth in the United States and also challenges common misunderstandings and stereotypes of the poor. It then presents a series of guidelines for action, including self-help programs for the poor, reevaluation of the tax code and reform of the welfare system.

The bishops address several issues related to food and agriculture. The nation's food production system is threatened with serious changes because of farm bankruptcies and the resulting concentration of land ownership. Modern agricultural practices are doing more and more damage to natural resources. World hunger continues in spite of food surpluses. Finally, the bishops express their concern about racial minorities, especially migratory field workers, who receive low wages and poor housing, health care and education. In response to these issues, the pastoral letter recommends specific policies that would help preserve moderate-sized farms operated by families, promote effective stewardship of soil and water and defend the dignity and fundamental rights of farm workers.

Following the tradition of Catholic social teaching, *Economic Justice for All* considers the global economy from the perspective of human dignity, justice and the common good. Although the social teaching does not demand absolute equality of wealth, it does challenge the shocking inequality between the rich and the poor. And shocking inequality exists in our world: At least eight hundred million people live below any rational definition of human decency; four hundred fifty million are chronically hungry and millions who survive are physically or mentally stunted.

NEEDED REFORMS

Because of its wealth and power, the United States has a primary role in reforming the international economic order, particularly in relation to the Third World. It must work with other influential nations, with multilateral institutions and with transnational banks and corporations. *Economic Justice for All* reviews five major areas where reform is needed and possible: (1) development assistance through grants, low-interest loans and technical aid; (2) trade policy that is especially sensitive to the poorest nations; (3) international finance and investment, with special attention to the Third World debt crisis; (4) private investment in foreign countries; (5) an international food system that increases immediate food aid and develops long-term programs to combat hunger.

The bishops acknowledge that their suggested reforms would be expensive. They also point to the immense human and social costs if reforms are not made. They judge that the amount of money (three hundred billion dollars a year) spent on military purposes should be reduced and some of this money directed toward social and economic reforms. And so they urge a new American experiment to complete the bold experiment in democracy begun more than two hundred years ago. This new experiment in economic justice will demand a greater spirit of partnership and teamwork, a renewed commitment to the common good.

The bishops end their long letter by reflecting on the Christian vocation and on the challenges to the church. The secular cannot be separated from the sacred. The Christian vocation means loving God and neighbor concretely in ways that transform society, in deeds of justice and service. The church itself is a major economic actor, with many employees, investments and properties. And so the bishops commit themselves to making the church a model of economic justice.

TEN YEARS LATER

To mark the tenth anniversary of *Economic Justice for All*, the bishops issued a very brief document, *A Catholic Framework for Economic Life*. The ten principles set out therein echo the much longer pastoral letter, highlighting again that the economy exists for the person. At a time of political posturing and powerful economic interests, the bishops focus on moral principles, the needs of the weak, the importance of the common good. For example, the last principle states: "The global economy has moral dimensions and human consequences. Decisions on investment, trade, aid and development should protect human life and promote human rights, especially for those most in need wherever they might live on this globe."

Archbishop Rembert Weakland also noted the anniversary with his lecture *"Economic Justice for All:* Ten Years Later." Weakland, who had chaired the committee that wrote the pastoral letter, reflects on how the letter would be different if it were written ten years later. His reflections emphasize a number of points, including the impact of the fall of communism, the globalization of the economy (this "would be the lens under which the other factors would be examined"), the necessary and proper role of government, the growing disparity between rich and poor. Weakland's comments on communism, capitalism and Catholic social teaching are particularly sober and realistic. After the fall of communism, he states, many economists felt that the free market system had won because of its inherent superiority. Despite Pope John Paul II's concerns about consumerism, exploitation and marginalization, critique of the limits of capitalism simply has not happened. Indeed, proponents of free-market economy even co-opted John Paul's encyclical (*On the Hundredth Anniversary of Rerum Novarum*) to support their own position. Weakland himself acknowledges that he now simply accepts as given fact the free-market economy. But he adds: "There will always be a tension between the Bible and capitalism, the Sermon on the Mount and the marketplace. The capitalist system is now accepted as a given in church documents since that is the world in which we all must live, but the defects and dangers in that system are also clearly pointed out."

GLOBALIZATION

In the years following Archbishop Weakland's remarks about globalization, the impact of and debate about globalization has increased significantly. "Neoliberal globalization" is a term frequently used to describe the dominant economic model, a model based on free markets and free trade. This neoliberal view stresses privatization, decreased regulation by governments, the lowering of barriers to international trade. In developed countries much emphasis is placed on its promise of economic prosperity for all. Perspectives from the developing world often highlight Weakland's comment about "defects and dangers."

A striking example of the latter view comes from Jesuit leaders of Latin America, rooted in their actual experience and in their commitment to the church's social teachings. They list some of the destructive results:

> ...the immense imbalances and perturbations neoliberalism causes through the concentration of income, wealth and land ownership; the multiplication of the unemployed urban masses or those surviving in unstable and unproductive jobs;

the bankruptcy of thousands of small- and medium-sized businesses; the destruction and forced displacement of indigenous and peasant populations; the expansion of drug trafficking based in rural sectors whose traditional products can no longer compete; the disappearance of food security; and increase in criminality often triggered by hunger; the destabilization of national economies by the free flow of international speculation; and maladjustments in local communities by multinational companies that do not take the residents into account.

In a number of his addresses, Pope John Paul II has also expressed a strong critique of neoliberal globalization. Of particular concern to John Paul was the growing gap between rich and poor countries, along with the undermining of human dignity. He stated that "various places are witnessing a resurgence of a certain capitalist neoliberalism that subordinates the human person to blind market forces" with the result that "the wealthy grow ever wealthier, while the poor grow ever poorer."

Pope John Paul II expresses concerns similar to those of the Jesuits, while ominously adding several more.

Special interests and the demands of the market frequently predominate over concern for the common good. This tends to leave the weaker members of society without adequate protection and can subject entire peoples and cultures to a formidable struggle for survival.

Moreover, it is disturbing to witness a globalization that exacerbates the conditions of the needy, that does not sufficiently contribute to resolving situations of hunger, poverty, and social inequality, that fails to safeguard the natural environment. These aspects of globalization can give rise to extreme reactions, leading to excessive nationalism, religious fanaticism and even acts of terrorism. (*Effective Mechanisms for Giving Globalization Proper Direction: Address to Pontifical Academy of Social Sciences*, 2003)

This long list of the dangers and defects of the dominant model of economic globalization, expressed by religious leaders and other critics of neoliberalism, may surprise many people in the developed world. Perhaps without even being aware of it, these people have internalized the market values of their society (see *Still Following Christ in a Consumer Society* by John Kavanaugh). Gospel values, as developed and applied by the social teachings, may seem idealistic and out of touch with reality—or simply be rejected as some form of communism or socialism.

Globalization, then, presents a profound challenge not only to economic justice but also to Christian living. "Economic and political decisions that are made concerning the shape of globalization," writes John Sniegocki, "will have a major impact on the lives of billions of the world's poor and will directly or indirectly affect all persons in an increasingly interconnected world. These choices may also determine the very fate of the earth itself."

Sniegocki offers a thoughtful analysis of globalization and its challenges, along with a realistic response grounded in Catholic social teachings. He discusses several points not yet mentioned, including neoliberal globalization's links to Third World debt and structural adjustment policies and to the International Monetary Fund and the World Bank. These policies and institutions have actually had a harsh impact on many poor people in the developing world, for example, by demanding production for export rather than for local needs. This focus contributes to increased hunger and malnutrition. Other pressures to meet debt payments lead to decreased budgets for education and health care.

Key themes from the social teachings—development of the whole person, solidarity, human rights, ecological concern—provide the foundations for an alternative model for globalization. Sniegocki sees local and national governments fostering the common good, along with the need for regulations to govern transnational corporations. This alternative approach would also include substantial debt relief and encourage economic democracy, prevent excessive disparities of wealth, and especially promote grassroots participation. Significantly, Sniegocki gives numerous examples of such a model actually working in the real world, including the Grameen Bank in Bangladesh and Kenya's Greenbelt Movement.

Still, if there is to be widespread success, Sniegocki states, then the church's proclamation of the social teachings must "more unambiguously encourage grassroots action and put this encouragement into practice at the parish level." Recognizing that such an approach will also face profound even violent resistance from the powers that be, Sniegocki counsels a deep commitment to nonviolence and respect for one's opponents.

A CONSISTENT ETHIC OF LIFE

In this chapter we have been considering many of the major social dilemmas of our day, a few in detail. These problems, so very much part of the real world, may seem to be overwhelming. We may ask what one person can do. Or, because many of us are among the rich (at least by comparison to millions of people around the world), we may feel guilty. While there may be appropriate times for this response, guilt may also limit our actions by paralyzing us. In its place honest realism and faithful responsibility lead to creative responses and effective action. As individuals we vote, develop and hand on attitudes about social issues, choose careers, participate in political and economic aspects of society. Here, concretely, we respond to the social issues.

As individuals, we are limited. So the recent social teachings have especially emphasized interdependence and solidarity. The issues of human rights, the economy and war are all interrelated. The social teachings challenge us to develop this global sensitivity. Beyond this awareness they also challenge us to work together. Individuals cannot do it all alone. In solidarity with others, people can create a new world.

In the last three chapters, we have reflected on a wide range of moral issues. Some of these are very intimate, some are global. In individual lives, some issues are undoubtedly more significant than others. Yet, whatever the issue—those included here or all those not discussed—it is in response to these moral dilemmas that we take a stand toward life, that we create the person we are becoming, that we answer God's call. In answering "What ought I/we to do?" we in fact answer "What ought I/we to be?"

A particular focus that holds together so many of these issues and questions is the consistent ethic of life. The late Cardinal Joseph Bernardin first articulated this perspective in the early 1980s as he worked to bring together those seeking an end to abortion and those trying to prevent nuclear war.

Already in his first lecture on the consistent ethic of life, he realized that commitment to life cannot be limited to one or two issues but must extend across the whole life span. From womb to tomb, life must be protected, nourished and cherished. He stated:

> If one contends, as we do, that the right of every fetus to be born should be protected by civil law and supported by civil consensus, then our moral, political and economic responsibilities do not stop at the moment of birth. Those who defend the right to life of the weakest among us must be equally visible in support of the quality of life of the powerless among us: the old and the young, the hungry and the homeless, the undocumented immigrant and the unemployed worker. Such a quality of life posture translates into specific political and economic positions on tax policy, employment generation, welfare policy, nutrition and feeding programs, and health care. Consistency means we cannot have it both ways. We cannot urge a compassionate society and vigorous public policy to protect the rights of the unborn and then argue that compassion and significant public programs on behalf of the needy undermine the moral fiber of the society or are beyond the proper scope of governmental responsibility. (*Consistent Ethic of Life*)

Although this linking of issues has not always been popular with particular interest groups, the consistent ethic of life has become the centerpiece of American Catholic moral teaching. This life ethic does not easily fit an existing category. It appears "liberal" on some issues, "conservative" on others. It challenges Republicans, Democrats and independents to promote life in all issues. It confronts believers, calling them to live gospel values more faithfully and authentically in all aspects of their lives.

Although Pope John Paul II did not use the phrase, his encyclical *The Gospel of Life* strongly affirms the consistent ethic of life. John Paul begins his letter by reflecting on the Cain and Abel story in the book of Genesis. This meditation provides the context for the pope's description of what is going on in our world today. What is going on is a monumental abuse of life: war and arms, drugs, destruction of the environment, abortion, euthanasia, unjust distribution of resources. This abuse is often caused and supported by the economic, social and political structures of the nations. So the pope speaks of a "structure of sin" and a "culture of death." Over against this culture of death, the pope wants to promote a culture of life. Indeed, the encyclical invites us all to choose life—consistently, personally, nationally, globally. This invitation is really a profound challenge: to look deeply into ourselves and to test against the gospel some deeply held beliefs and practices. *The Gospel of Life* calls us to be consistent—to be pro-life in all the issues, not just some. It calls us to be personally committed, willing to bear the cost of discipleship. It calls us to be involved, to help our nation affirm human dignity and justice throughout the world.

As we enter a new millennium, world events and church teachings direct our attention to life itself as the very center of our concern. The consistent ethic of life provides both a solid foundation and a powerful challenge to live as faithful disciples and involved citizens. The consistent ethic of life urges us to speak and act concerning abortion and euthanasia but also concerning welfare and immigration, sexism and racism, genetics and health-care reform, trade agreements, genocide and terrorism, war and many other issues. Based on our ancient Scriptures and attentive to contemporary experiences, the consistent ethic of life provides an ethical framework for confronting the moral dilemmas of a new millennium and for promoting the full flourishing of all life.

CATECHISM REFERENCES
Nos. 1897–1948, 2234–2246, 2302–2317, 2401–2463.

FOR REFLECTION AND DISCUSSION

1. As you reflect on a hundred years of social teaching, do you find some themes especially important for your own life? Are human dignity, participation in creating your future and social justice realities in your life? How are they helped or hindered by your work, by life in the church and in our culture?

2. Is there a necessary relationship between morality and politics or should the bishops stay out of politics? How do your political views match those recommended by the bishops? What are your reasons for agreeing or disagreeing? How does all this relate to the chapter on conscience and authority?

3. Many issues are both local and global. How can you get involved in the debate over public policy about these issues? What can ordinary citizens do besides vote? How does the "consistent ethic of life" fit in the voting booth?

4. Have you or someone you know experienced racism, sexism, homelessness, the need for welfare? How has this experience influenced your life? In light of that experience, how do you react to the bishops' convictions about political responsibility?

5. What is your response to the bishops' position on deterrence? Do you think nuclear war is likely in your lifetime? How can it be prevented? Where do you see the faces of violence? In your home and community, how can you foster a spirit of nonviolence and patiently construct peace?

6. Do you know anyone directly affected by terrorism or war? What sources of information do you rely on for knowledge about these issues? How is this related to conscience and the search for truth described in chapter three? What are the relationships between economic structures and policies, terrorism and war?

7. What are some of the strengths and benefits of the economy in your local community? What are some of the ugly realities? What has been your experience of these goods and evils? What can the preferential option for the poor mean for you and your local community? Reflect on your own sense of the meaning of global interdependence and of the common good. How can your economic decisions respect these worldwide concerns?

8. Although it was not discussed in detail in this book, the environment is another issue that relates to the survival of the planet. What are the major environmental issues facing your local community, the nation, the world? What actions have already been taken concerning these issues? How can you help in your local area?

9. *The Gospel of Life* is a bold and prophetic proclamation that invites you to look deeply within yourself and our society. What are the basic values, and where do they come from? What is life, its meaning and value? Can you praise the good in the American way of life but also honestly acknowledge how it is a culture of death? How can you express your convictions in concrete actions?

Bibliography

Contemporary Moral Theology

Barnett, William R., Robert F. Kelly and William C. Rinaman. "What American Catholics Think About the Scandal." *Conversations on Jesuit Higher Education*, Number 26, Fall 2004, pp. 23–26.

Beal, John P. "Hiding in the Thickets of the Law." *America*, October 7, 2002, pp. 15–19.

Cahill, Lisa Sowle, and James Childress, eds. *Christian Ethics: Problems and Prospects*. Cleveland: The Pilgrim Press, 1996.

Connors, Russell B., Jr., and Patrick McCormick. *Character, Choices & Community*. Mahwah, N.J.: Paulist Press, 1998.

Cozzens, Donald B. *Sacred Silence: Denial and the Crisis in the Church*. Collegeville, Minn.: Liturgical Press, 2002.

Curran, Charles, and Richard McCormick, S.J., eds. *Readings in Moral Theology* (numerous volumes). Mahwah, N.J.: Paulist Press, 1979 and later.

Dulles, Cardinal Avery, S.J. "Rights of Accused Priests." *America*, June 21–28, 2004, pp. 19–23.

Editors. "Healing and Credibility." *America*, April 1, 2002, p. 3

Flannery, Austin, O.P., ed. *Vatican Council II: The Basic Sixteen Documents* (in inclusive language). Northport, N.Y.: Costello Publishing Company, 1996.

Flynn, Archbishop Harry J. "What Has the Charter Accomplished?" *America*, October 18, 2004, pp. 8–11.

Fogarty, Gerald P., S.J. "The American Catholic Tradition of Dialogue." *America*, October 26, 1996, pp. 9–14.

Gregory, Bishop Wilton. "Presidential Address." *Origins*, Vol. 32, No. 7, June 27, 2002, pp. 97–102.

Gula, Richard, S.S. *The Call to Holiness*. Mahwah, N.J.: Paulist Press, 2003.

———. *The Good Life*. Mahwah, N.J.: Paulist Press, 1999.

———. *Reason Informed By Faith*. Mahwah, N.J.: Paulist Press, 1989.

Gustafson, James. *Protestant and Roman Catholic Ethics*. Chicago: The University of Chicago Press, 1978.

Häring, Bernard. *Free and Faithful in Christ*. New York: Seabury Press, 1978.

Harrington, Daniel, S.J., and James Keenan, S.J. *Jesus and Virtue Ethics*. Lanham, Md.: Sheed & Ward, 2002.

Hauerwas, Stanley. *A Community of Character*. Notre Dame: University of Notre Dame Press, 1981.

Kammer, Charles L., III. *Ethics and Liberation*. Maryknoll, N.Y.: Orbis Books, 1988.

Keenan, James F., S.J. "Ethics and the Crisis in the Church." *Theological Studies*, Vol. 66, No. 1, March 2005, pp. 117–136.

_____. *Virtues for Ordinary Christians*. Franklin, Wis.: Sheed & Ward, 1999.

Mahoney, John, S.J. *The Making of Moral Theology*. New York: Oxford University Press, 1987.

McCormick, Richard, S.J. *Ambiguity in Moral Choice*. Milwaukee, Wis.: Marquette University Press, 1973.

_____. *Notes on Moral Theology, 1965–1980*. Washington, D.C.: University Press of America, 1981.

_____. *Notes on Moral Theology, 1981–1984*. Lanham, Md.: University Press of America, 1984.

Monden, Louis, S.J. *Sin, Liberty, and Law*. Kansas City, Mo.: Sheed & Ward, 1965.

National Conference of Catholic Bishops. *Human Life in Our Day*. Washington, D.C.: USCC Office of Publishing Services, 1968.

National Pastoral Life Center. "Called to Be Catholic: Church in a Time of Peril." *America*, August 31, 1996, pp. 5–8.

O'Connell, Timothy. *Principles for a Catholic Morality*, rev. ed. New York: HarperCollins, 1990.

O'Donovan, Leo, S.J., ed. *A World of Grace*. New York: Crossroad, 1987.

O'Malley, John W., S.J. "The Scandal: A Historian's Perspective." *America*, May 27, 2002, pp. 14–17.

Overberg, Kenneth, S.J. *Roots and Branches*, rev. ed. Kansas City, Mo.: Sheed & Ward, 1991.

Porter, Jean. *The Recovery of Virtue*. Louisville: Westminster/John Knox Press, 1990.

Quinn, Archbishop John R. "The Exercise of the Papacy." *Commonweal*, July 12, 1996, pp. 11–20.

_____. "Considerations for a Church in Crisis." *America*, May 27, 2002, pp. 10–11.

Rahner, Karl, S.J. *Foundations of Christian Faith*. New York: Seabury Press, 1978.

_____. *Theological Investigations*. New York: Helicon Press, 1961. (See especially articles in volumes 2, 4, 6, 9 and 20.)

Rausch, Thomas, S.J. "The Lay Vocation and Voice of the Faithful." *America*, September 29, 2003, pp. 8–11.

Spohn, William C. *Go and Do Likewise*. New York: Continuum, 2003.

Steinfels, Margaret O'Brien. "The Church and Its Public Life." *America*, June 10, 1989, pp. 550–558.

Steinfels, Peter. *A People Adrift: The Crisis of the Roman Catholic Church in America*. New York: Simon and Schuster, 2003.

Sullivan, Francis, S.J. *Magisterium*. Mahwah, N.J.: Paulist Press, 1983.

United States Conference of Catholic Bishops. "Charter for the Protection of Children and Young People" with "Essential Norms" (revised). *Origins*, Vol. 32, No. 25, November 28, 2002, pp. 409–418.

Wilkins, John, ed. *Considering Veritatis Splendor*. Cleveland: The Pilgrim Press, 1994.

Winters, Michael Sean. "The Betrayal." *The New Republic*, May 6, 2002, pp. 24–27.

Contemporary Moral Issues

Ashley, Benedict, O.P., and Kevin O'Rourke, O.P. *Healthcare Ethics*, 3rd ed. St. Louis: The Catholic Health Association of the United States, 1989.

Bernardin, Cardinal Joseph. *Consistent Ethic of Life*. Kansas City, Mo.: Sheed & Ward, 1988.

_____. *A Moral Vision for America* (John P. Langan, S.J., ed.). Washington, D.C.: Georgetown University Press, 1998.

_____. "Managing Managed Care." *Origins*, Vol. 26, No. 2, May 30, 1996, pp. 21–26.

Bonneau, Normand, et al. *AIDS and Faith*. Ottawa: Novalis, 1993.

Bresnahan, James F., S.J. "Killing vs. Letting Die: A Moral Distinction Before the Courts." *America*, February 1, 1997, pp. 8–16.

Byock, Ira, M.D. *Dying Well*. New York: Riverhead Books, 1997.

Byron, William J., S.J. "Catholic Health Care: Partnering and Progress." *America*, September 28, 1996, pp. 16–21.

Cahill, Lisa Sowle. "Catholicism, Death and Modern Medicine." *America*, April 25, 2005, pp. 14–17.

_____. "Realigning Catholic Priorities: Bioethics and the Common Good." *America*, September 13, 2004, pp. 11–13.

Callahan, Daniel. "Allocating Health Resources." *Hastings Center Report*, April/May, 1988, pp. 14–20.

Callahan, Sydney. "A Feminist Case Against Euthanasia." *Health Progress*, November-December, 1996, pp. 21–29.

Cavanaugh, John, et al. *Alternatives to Economic Globalization: A Better World Is Possible.* San Francisco: Berrett-Koehler, 2002.

Childress, James. "Who Shall Live When Not All Can Live?" *Bioethics*, rev. ed., Thomas Shannon, ed. Mahwah, N.J.: Paulist Press, 1981.

Christiansen, Drew, S.J. "On Many Things." *America*, September 13, 2004, p. 2.

———. "Whither the 'Just War'?" *America*, March 24, 2003, pp. 7–11.

Coleman, Gerald D., S.S. *Homosexuality.* Mahwah, N.J.: Paulist Press, 1995.

Council on Ethical and Judicial Affairs of the American Medical Association. "Ethical Issues in Managed Care." *The Journal of the American Medical Association*, Vol. 273, No. 4, January 25, 1995, pp. 330–335.

Dent, Martin and Bill Peters. *The Crisis of Poverty and Debt in the Third World.* Aldershot, Hampshire, U.K.: Ashgate, 1999.

Devine, Richard J. *Good Care, Painful Choices: Medical Ethics for Ordinary People,* third ed. Mahwah, N.J.: Paulist Press, 2004.

Editors with Lisa Sowle Cahill and Michael Baxter, C.S.C. "Is This Just War?" *U.S. Catholic*, December 2001, pp. 13–16.

Fuller, Jon, S.J. "AIDS Prevention: A Challenge to the Catholic Moral Tradition." *America*, December 28, 1996, pp. 13–20.

Gibbons, William, ed. *Seven Great Encyclicals.* Mahwah, N.J.: Paulist Press, 1963.

Gremillion, Joseph. *The Gospel of Peace and Justice.* Maryknoll, N.Y.: Orbis Books, 1976.

Hamel, Ronald and Michael Panicola. "Must We Preserve Life?" *America*, April 19–26, 2004, pp. 6–13.

Haughey, John, S.J., ed. *The Faith That Does Justice.* Mahwah, N.J.: Paulist Press, 1977.

Hollenbach, David, S.J. "Responding to the Terrorist Attacks: An Ethical Perspective." *America*, October 22, 2001, pp. 23–24.

Hurrell, Andrew and Ngaire Woods, eds. *Inequality, Globalization, and World Politics.* New York: Oxford University Press, 2000.

Irwin, Alexander, Joyce Millen and Dorothy Fallows. *Global AIDS: Myths and Facts.* Cambridge, Mass.: South End Press, 2003.

Jesuit Provincials of Latin America. "For Life and Against Neoliberalism." *We Make the Road by Walking*, Ann Butwell, Kathy Ogle, Scott Wright, eds. Washington, D.C.: EPICA, 1998.

John Paul II. "Care for Patients in a Permanent Vegetative State." *Origins*, Vol. 33, No. 42, April 8, 2004, pp. 737–740.

_____. "A Church Responding to the Sick and the Poor in Burundi." *Origins*, Vol. 20, No. 15, September 20, 1990, pp. 243–245.

_____. "Effective Mechanisms for Giving Globalization Proper Direction: Address to the Pontifical Academy of Social Sciences." *Origins*, Vol. 33, No. 2, May 22, 2003, pp. 29–30.

_____. *The Gospel of Life*. Washington, D.C.: USCC Office of Publishing Services, 1995.

_____. "Homily in Cuba" (on globalization). *We Make the Road by Walking*, Ann Butwell, Kathy Ogle, Scott Wright, eds. Washington, D.C.: EPICA, 1998.

_____. *On Human Work*. Washington, D.C.: USCC Office of Publishing Services, 1981.

_____. *On the Hundredth Anniversary of Rerum Novarum*. Washington, D.C.: USCC Office of Publishing Services, 1991.

_____. "The International Situation Today: Address to the Diplomatic Corps." *Origins*, Vol. 32, No. 33, January 30, 2003, pp. 543–545.

_____. "Message for World Peace Day." *America*, January 7–14, 2002, pp. 7–11.

_____. *On Social Concern*. Washington, D.C.: USCC Office of Publishing Services, 1987.

Kavanaugh, John. *Still Following Christ in a Consumer Society*. Maryknoll, N.Y.: Orbis Books, 1991.

Kaveny, M. Cathleen. "Assisted Suicide, Euthanasia, and the Law." *Theological Studies*, Vol. 58, No. 1, March 1997, pp. 124–148.

Keane, Philip S. *Health Care Reform: A Catholic View*. Mahwah, N.J.: Paulist Press, 1993.

Keenan, James F., S.J., ed. *Catholic Ethicists on HIV/AIDS Prevention*. New York: Continuum, 2000.

_____. "The Open Debate: Moral Theology and the Lives of Gay and Lesbian Persons." *Theological Studies*, Vol. 64, No. 1, March 2003, pp. 127–150.

Kim, Jim Yong, Joyce Millen, Alec Irwin, and John Gershman, eds. *Dying for Growth: Global Inequality and the Health of the Poor*. Monroe, Me.: Common Courage Press, 2000.

Mann, Jonathan, Daniel J.M. Tarantola and Thomas W. Netter, eds. *AIDS in the World*. Cambridge, Mass.: Harvard University Press, 1992.

Mariner, Wendy K. "Business vs. Medical Ethics: Conflicting Standards for Managed Care." *Journal of Law, Medicine & Ethics*, 23 (1995), pp. 236–246.

McCormick, Richard, S.J. *The Critical Calling*. Washington, D.C.: Georgetown University Press, 1989.

_____. *Health and Medicine in the Catholic Tradition*. New York: Crossroad, 1984.

National Conference of Catholic Bishops. *Always Our Children*. Washington, D.C.: USCC Office of Publishing Services, 1998.

_____. *Called to Compassion and Responsibility*. Washington, D.C.: USCC Office of Publishing Services, 1989.

_____. *A Catholic Framework for Economic Life*. Washington, D.C.: USCC Office of Publishing Services, 1997.

_____. *The Challenge of Peace*. Washington, D.C.: USCC Office of Publishing Services, 1983.

_____. *Economic Justice for All*. Washington, D.C.: USCC Office of Publishing Services, 1986.

_____. *Ethical and Religious Directives for Catholic Health Care Services*. Washington, D.C.: USCC Office of Publishing Services, 2001.

_____. *Faithful for Life: A Moral Reflection*. Washington, D.C.: USCC Office of Publishing Services, 1995.

_____. *The Harvest of Justice Is Sown in Peace*. Washington, D.C.: USCC Office of Publishing Services, 1993.

_____. *The Many Faces of AIDS*. Washington, D.C.: USCC Office of Publishing Services, 1987.

_____. *Political Responsibility*. Washington, D.C.: USCC Office of Publishing Services, 1996.

_____. *To Live in Christ Jesus*. Washington, D.C.: USCC Office of Publishing Services, 1976.

Nugent, Robert and Jeannine Gramick. *Building Bridges: Gay & Lesbian Reality and the Catholic Church*. Mystic, Conn.: Twenty-Third Publications, 1992.

O'Brien, David, and Thomas Shannon, eds. *Renewing the Earth*. New York: Doubleday, 1977.

Ohio Catholic Conference of Bishops. *Hopes and Fears: Pastoral Reflections on Death*. Columbus: Catholic Conference of Ohio, 1993.

Outka, Gene. "Social Justice and Equal Access to Health Care." *Bioethics*, 3rd ed., Thomas Shannon, ed. Mahwah, N.J.: Paulist Press, 1987.

Overberg, Kenneth, S.J., ed. *AIDS, Ethics & Religion*. Maryknoll, N.Y.: Orbis Books, 1994.

_____. *Creating a Culture of Life*. Notre Dame, Ind.: Ave Maria Press, 2002.

_____. *An Inconsistent Ethic?* Lanham, Md.: University Press of America, 1980.

_____, ed. *Mercy or Murder? Euthanasia, Morality and Public Policy*. Kansas City,

Mo.: Sheed & Ward, 1993.

Panicola, Michael. "Catholic Teaching on Prolonging Life: Setting the Record Straight." *Hastings Center Report*, 31, November–December 2001, pp. 14–25.

Paterson, Gillian. *Women in the Time of AIDS*. Maryknoll, N.Y.: Orbis Books, 1996.

Rahner, Karl, s.j. *The Practice of Faith*. New York: Crossroad, 1986.

Ratzinger, Cardinal Joseph. "Letter to the Bishops of the Catholic Church on the Pastoral Care of Homosexual Persons." *Origins*, Vol. 16, No. 22, November 13, 1986, pp. 377–382.

Siker, Jeffrey S., ed. *Homosexuality in the Church: Both Sides of the Debate*. Louisville, Ky.: Westminster John Knox Press, 1994.

Sniegocki, John. "Catholic Social Teaching and Economic Globalization." Paper presented at the Lilly Research Fellows Conference on Christianity and Economics, Baylor University, November 2002.

United States Conference of Catholic Bishops. *Faithful Citizenship: A Catholic Call to Political Responsibility*. Washington, D.C.: USCC Office of Publishing Services, 2003.

_____. "Statement on Iraq." *Origins*, Vol. 32, No. 24, November 21, 2002, pp. 406–408.

Vatican (per Archbishop Celestino Migliore). "Preventing a Possible War in Iraq: Intervention in the Security Council of the United Nations." *Origins*, Vol. 32, No. 38, March 6, 2003, pp. 625–627.

Waters, Brent and Ronald Cole-Turner, eds. *God and the Embryo: Religious Voices on Stem Cells and Cloning*. Washington, D.C.: Georgetown University Press, 2003.

Weakland, Archbishop Rembert G., o.s.b. "*Economic Justice for All:* Ten Years Later." *America*, March 22, 1997, pp. 8–22.

Weigel, George. "The Just War Case for the War." *America*, March 31, 2003, pp. 7–10.

Wink, Walter. *Engaging the Powers*. Minneapolis: Fortress Press, 1992.

Wolf, Susan, ed. *Feminism & Bioethics: Beyond Reproduction*. New York: Oxford University Press, 1996.

Index

papal infallibility, 42
papal teachings, about birth control,
71–73
partial-birth abortion, 70
*Pastoral Constitution on the Church in the
Modern World,* 13, 14, 37
Paul VI, 45, 71, 72, 125
human development and, 114–115
peace
challenge of, 121–122
war and, 14, 117, 122–123
Peace on Earth (John XXIII), 112, 113, 114
pederasty, 63
personal lives, moral choices relating to,
xi, 3
personal relationships, xi
personal responsibility, 54
philosophy, transcendental method of, 15
physical integrity, 25
physician-assisted suicide. *See* assisted
suicide
Pius XI, 111, 112
Pius XII, 41, 111
pluralism, xi, 69, 103, 104, 118
polarization, 49
political responsibility, 119–121
voting as, 121
politics, moral choices about, xii, 3, 45
poor, rich v., 115, 117, 135
popes, 40, 41, 110
*Populorum Progressio. See The Development
of Peoples*
poverty, 70, 95, 98, 117, 120, 132–133
The Practice of Faith (Rahner), 61
preemptive war, xiv
pregnancy, 67–68
prejudice, 64
premoral and moral evil, 25–26, 28
principle of double effect, 31–32
Principles for a Catholic Morality (O'
Connell), 38
private property, 117
Prodigal Son, story of, 10
Promised Land, Canaan as, 8
"proportionate reason," xiii
prostitution, 63

Quinn, John R., 48–49, 52–53

racism, xi, 67, 70, 98, 100, 109, 140
Raffelt, Albert, 61
Rahner, Karl, 12, 15–18, 19, 46, 54–56,
61, 129
rape, 67
reality
as basis of morality, 4–7, 18, 21, 24
God, human beings, and rest of
creation, 5
of moral decision-making, 4–5, 35
reason, sufficient, presence or absence of,
25, 65–66
The Reconstruction of the Social Order (Pius
XI), 111
redemption, 11–12
reign, of God, 122, 131
relativism, xiv, 21, 54, 62
religious beliefs, 27
religious law, xi
reproductive technology, 80
Rerum Novarum. See The Condition of Labor
resources, scarce, use of. *See* scarce
resources and managed care
respirators, 86
responsibility
conscience and, 53–54
personal, 54
resurrection, of Jesus, 10, 11, 84
rich, poor v., 115, 117, 135
right course of action, search for, 38, 53
"right to die," 83
rights
human, 112–114, 117, 138
of women, 67, 68–69
of workers, 111, 117
"Rights of Accused Priests" (Dulles), 52
Roe v. Wade, 68, 69
Roman Catechism, xiii
Roman Catholic moral theology, xiv, 64
Roman Curia, 48, 49
Roman Pontiff, 43
Romero, Oscar, 46
Russia. *See* Soviet Union

salvation, God's desire for, 12